JEREMY WOODWARD'S

Story of

HEART FAILURE TO VICTORY

Todd,
Dream. Believe. Inspire.

Heart Failure to Victory

For more information, please contact:
Clvin Media Relations,
2 Robbins Rd, Winchendon, MA 01475
978-502-1453

Library of Congress Control Number:
ISBN-13: 978-0-578-80734-8

Cover Photo: Joanna Puza
Cover design: Callie Cole

We dedicate this book, with love…

To my Dad; my role model, mentor, and inspiration.

J.W.

To Cole; You're going to do great things. I love you.

B.V.

Throughout my entire life, my father has been my inspiration. He has set such an amazing example for everyone that has had the privilege of knowing him. Unfortunately, several months after the rough draft of this book was finished, he lost a long and hard battle with cancer. He embodied everything that I strive to be as a business owner. If I can be half of the parent he was, my kids will have the best father ever. Just as he did for me, I encourage anyone reading this to be a role model for someone. Family member, friend, coworker, child, it doesn't matter. He has had a lasting impact on me, and I plan to carry that leadership forward in everything I do. He lived life to the fittest, and I plan to do the same.

Chuck Woodward

March 8th, 1951 — May 23rd, 2015

Acknowledgements

It has been a dream come true to put this book together. I have wanted my story told and my journey shared with the world, and this book manages to do both beautifully. There are so many people to thank for making this happen. First, to Ben Veilleux, the brawn behind this whole thing. You took my thoughts, memories and experiences and put them to paper in a way I never thought possible. To my amazing friends Jay and Marshall, thank you for your input. Mr. Hardy, thank you for always being there for me and being the best role model anyone could ever ask for. A sincere thank you to the Bodyworks family of black belts for all of the bonds and memories we have. To Brook, Ellie, Bryn and Isla, thank you for being such a supportive and loving family. Todd Civin, thank you for pushing me to pursue this project. And lastly, thank you to all of the members of the cardiology teams at Tufts Medical Center and Boston Medical Center.

~ Jeremy Woodward

What a journey. Writing this book has been nothing short of a life-changing experience. First and foremost, I would like to give my sincerest thanks to Jeremy Woodward for providing the opportunity for this project. It may have taken six full years for this story to come together along with plenty of phone tag and stress, but it was worth it. To my editor-in-chief, there is no doubt that I would not be anywhere close to where I am today without your help, thanks Mom! To all who have helped with content editing (Jayla, David, Mike, Derek, Robyn, Laurie, Georgette, Alicia, Jonatha and Erin) your input has been incredibly helpful and valuable. A special thanks to Brook Woodward, thank you for allowing me to pick your brain all these times. Thank you to Marshall, Jay, and Mr. Hardy for your wonderful insight about Jeremy. You three, along with Brook, helped make this book stand out as something very special. To all of my friends and family that kept the encouragement train rolling, thank you all. Thank you to my wife, Mikayla, for all the support involved with the final legs of this work. And last, but most certainly not least, thank you to Mr. Curt McDermott for starting me down the path of authorship.

~ *Ben Veilleux*

Table of Contents

Foreword

I have known and worked with Jeremy since he was an adolescent. He became my karate student and soon began demonstrating what would turn out to be a long relationship of commitment, enthusiasm, success and friendship. Jeremy developed into a leader and role model early. He became an advanced martial arts instructor within my school, was consistently successful in competitions, and inspired others at demonstrations.

When Jeremy experienced heart failure it was devastating for all those who had surrounded him for years. I, like many others, reluctantly considered the unthinkable; an abrupt halt to his life of physical training, teaching, and his ongoing quest to conquer one mountain after another. It took a while for the shock to wear off and once we knew more of his situation, it was clear that he was in for the fight of his young life. Even with Jeremy's fortitude and inner strength, none of us knew what was going to happen.

It was soon apparent that Jeremy would not take this lying down (literally). He began to fight despite the agonizing months of treatment. He was the recipient of a tissue heart valve. What could that mean for someone with such an active history? Well, it meant work, work, and more work. Jeremy slowly began to re-emerge as the strong force he had previously been. He was making a comeback and it was incredible. But once again he was tested with the failure of the valve in his chest. This in fact was his next mountain.

At this point, all we could do is shake our heads and wonder, why? Well, Jeremy powered through this setback just as he had done initially. He made a vow that if he ever was physically able, and with medical clearance, he would pursue an Ironman competition…his way of making a statement about the power within.

In July of 2010, Jeremy did indeed compete in the Ironman competition at Lake Placid New York. After that, he began helping coordinate various triathlons and running events throughout the region, and focused on generating resources for a local, well deserving nature conservancy. His efforts and accomplishments drew attention and respect from individuals and groups within the medical, fitness, political, and promotional fields. It was no surprise that Jeremy's business flourished rapidly and became the perfect venue for him to lead others in their quest for better health. "*Living Life to the Fittest*" is Jeremy's message, and also depicts his level of passion. And what could be more enriching than being passionate and skillful at something that uplifts others. In Jeremy's case this brought him success as well.

Jeremy is an extraordinary man who has dealt with extraordinary challenges. His enthusiasm and "game on" attitude in approaching every project he sets his sights on evokes the warrior spirit within us all and is a testament to the inner qualities we are responsible for striving toward.

Jeff Hardy
Director / Bodyworks Martial Arts School
Emergency Services Clinician
MS, Licensed Clinical Mental Health Counselor

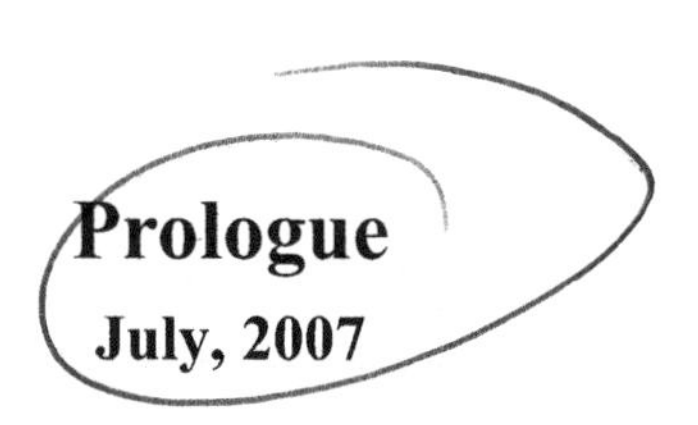

Prologue

July, 2007

Rays of sunlight sliced through the partly cloudy sky, making me squint involuntarily. I marveled at the beauty. The beams of sunlight streaming down resembled massive scythes, cutting through the cotton-like clouds at abstract angles. The clouds themselves moved lazily across the endless blue, morphing constantly. Every now and then I was able to discern shapes and figures out of the clouds.

Though we are all exposed to these sights on a regular basis, I was looking at the horizon through a new set of eyes and with a new appreciation of my surroundings. The trees swaying ever so slightly in the breeze, the hawk coasting on the wind currents above, the feel of the midsummer warmth against my skin; all these sensory experiences seemed extraordinary at that time.

The date was July 21st, 2007. The UV index was 9, a high level even for summer in New England. However, the comfortable temperature of seventy degrees made the heat quite bearable. Despite the beautiful weather the mood was anything but cheery. We were driving to Tufts Medical Center in order to learn how to treat what had been plaguing me for the past several months. My wife and I knew I was in the worst stage of heart failure. I was carrying forty pounds of excess fluid. As my wife drove I could feel her glancing worriedly at me from time to time. I couldn't bear to meet her gaze.

The clouds above, which had previously seemed sluggish, parted in haste and sunlight cascaded through as if a faucet had just been thrown open. The suddenness forced my eyes shut even further. I fought through the urge to squint and stared up into the sky, wondering if I would soon be making a venture beyond the clouds and into the heavens.

The hour-long drive from New Hampshire turned into almost three times that, although anyone that has driven in Boston can surely attest to having similar experiences. The pleasant summer air had given way to a muggy, almost damp feel to the atmosphere in downtown Boston. After multiple references to a street map and with a stroke of luck, we finally found the parking garage for Tufts. Brook accepted the stub at the ticket window and sped further into the garage. The first few rows of parking spots were completely full, as we expected. After she saw that the entire first floor was full, Brook hurriedly drove up to the second floor, only to see it too was packed. Even the third floor was full. Rather than go higher and make it a longer walk, she decided to circle back around and go back down to the lower floors.

That driving in the garage felt like an eternity. I was exhausted, drained of energy and devoid of emotion. My head was braced against the window at an uncomfortable angle that hurt my neck, but I was too tired to shift my position. I gazed out at the different colors of cars and trucks that we passed. The odd rainbow of colors from the vehicles that played out in front of me allowed me to zone out, the first time that day that I wasn't dwelling on my state and the variables that lay ahead. Mercifully, after ten minutes that felt like a lifetime, we found a parking spot on the first level.

I glanced out the window in the direction of the entrance. I estimated we were about one hundred yards from the doors. 'I can do this,' I thought to myself. 'Only a short walk and I'm good.' Brook came around to my side of the car, opened the door and offered her hands. I winced as my back muscles reminded me that I hadn't moved in over an hour. With lots of assistance from Brook I managed to get out of the car, bracing myself against the hood as she closed the door and came back around to further assist me.

We were running late for my appointment. Brook had called the medical center on the drive down to tell them we were slightly behind schedule. I lifted my head and stared at the hospital doors. Though it was only a hundred yards, the distance from the doors to where I stood seemed to be miles. With one hand on my wrist and the other wrapped around me, Brook took a tentative step toward the doors, silently urging me forward. I grimaced and followed. A hundred yards is not a long distance for most people to walk. However, when one is dying of heart failure, has an empty stomach and is carrying forty pounds of excess fluid on their body, you'd better believe that walking any distance is a challenge in and of itself. Those hundred yards were the longest I have ever traveled in my life.

Every step was a chore. Every shuffle was excruciating. Every second was harder than the last. Sure, a wheelchair would have been much easier and faster, but anyone who knows me knows that I am far too stubborn to accept that kind of help. 'This is *my* life, *my* condition, *my* journey,' I thought to myself, and walking to that door without the aid of a wheelchair was something I needed to do on my own.

It must have taken a full ten minutes to walk from the car to those doors, and sensing my presence, they silently slid open, a hint of disinfectant and air freshener escaping the entryway. I had made it. I was at the medical center. The clean scent of the hospital wafted into my lungs. Now we could finally find out how to treat my condition. Taking a deep breath, I continued to put one foot in front of the other and entered the building, unaware that I was about to embark on the most unlikely journey of my life.

Three Years Later…

The crisp night air rushed through my hair as the lights of the city came closer and closer. Each footstep brought the cheering crowds closer. My feet felt like bricks, but I was past the point of noticing fatigue; I had mentally blocked out the screaming of my muscles twenty miles ago. My new friend that I was running with commented on the sight of the stars shining above us in a clear night sky. The moonlight illuminated our path, showing that we had a straight shot into the city. We had just over one mile and we'd be there.

Before I knew it, the roaring of the crowd welcomed us into the city, so strong that we could physically feel it. When we had just under a mile to go, my favorite song started playing through the many speakers spread out along the finish line. I chuckled, shook my head in disbelief and knew this was it. Over a hundred and thirty miles so far that day, and it had all led up to this. I took in a deep breath and pushed it right back out, allowing myself to get amped up. I shrugged my shoulders and drew upon every last ounce of energy I had left. I had come so far since being hospitalized and unable to move, on the brink of death. Now I was here, running the race of my life. 'I've never felt so alive,' I thought to myself. With that thought, I kicked it into overdrive and started my final push to the finish line.

Part One: Adolescence, Martial Arts & Heart Scans, oh my!

Chapter One
My Introduction to a Martial Arts Lifestyle

My arms were starting to falter under the weight of the bar. The strain on my muscles was taking its toll. I could see my biceps writhing beneath my skin. 'Three more presses,' I told myself. "One, two!" I gasped through ragged breaths. I was almost there! With an audible groan of effort, I thrust the bar off my chest and into the air for a final time. My spotter took over and placed the bar back into a resting position. I hoisted myself off the bench, proud of the feat I had just accomplished. For weeks I had been working toward increasing the amount of weight I could bench press for ten reps. Through many hours of physical exertion and just as much patience, I had done it. I couldn't help smiling. As my breathing started to return to normal, my gaze traveled across the room and settled on the reflection of the room in the mirror.

My light blonde hair glistened with sweat. I was squinting to save my eyes from being stung by the dripping perspiration. A dark stain had soaked into the neck of my tank top, which I used to wipe off my brow. My chest was rippling, still recovering from the bench presses. I took another look around the room. There were about ten others scattered throughout the weight room. At fourteen years old, I was the youngest in the room. A massive middle-aged man in the corner was curling an ungodly amount of weight. Another was leg pressing five times his weight. Yet another was squatting a bar that dwarfed my bench press weight. This display of size and strength did not intimidate me. On the contrary, it gave me motivation, a desire to further enhance my own level of fitness.

A loud shout from the other room startled me, piquing my curiosity. I moved to the window to take a look. What I saw through that thin pane of glass made my eyes go wide with excitement.

A martial arts class was underway. The gym, called 'the den', was in the same facility as a martial arts school, both owned and operated by the same individual. It was a small class, about six or seven people wearing similar gi tops, all with black belts adorning their waists. My eyes were drawn to the two people in the middle of the room. One was a young man I guessed to be in his mid-twenties. The other was a behemoth of a man, probably in his thirties. His arms were monstrous. He had jet-black hair that he wore in a mullet and an equally long handlebar moustache. His face bore a relaxed and calm expression, which was odd to me, seeing as the other man was actively striking at him. Punches and kicks were being thrown at the man with the large arms, but he remained relaxed as he blocked, parried, bumped or passed every strike. Not one strike made contact with its intended target.

Without warning, the large man who had been on defense caught the other man's fist mid-punch. Before the offensive man knew what had occurred, he was on the ground and tapping out from a joint manipulation. I shook my head, taken aback by what I had just witnessed. In the blink of an eye, the defensive man had taken the attacker down and made him tap out with what seemed like no effort.

The larger man helped his partner up and turned to address the other students. He was clearly the person running the class. He spoke with an authoritative air, exuding confidence and knowledge with every word. The others in the room were hanging on everything he said. I scanned the audience. Not one set of eyes wavered, no one seemed anything short of completely plugged in to what he had to say. From a cue that I couldn't hear, the class split into groups of two and started working back and forth with what looked like a prescribed drill. There were people of all physical shapes and sizes: large, built guys were standing next to much smaller women, who were next to short, compact men. Even more interesting was that the students didn't pair off by size at all, but seemingly randomly.

For example, a large bodybuilder was paired with a tall, lanky individual directly on the other side of the glass. The larger of the two was the one striking. I forced myself to withhold a laugh. 'The small guy doesn't stand a chance!' I thought. To my astonishment, the lanky student took the bodybuilder down to the ground with just as much ease and speed as the teacher had. I was intrigued. Actually, I take that back. Forget intrigued, I was absolutely hooked! "Amazing!" I said out loud to myself.

"You think so?" said a voice from behind me. I barely caught a scream of fright from escaping past my lips as I whirled around. The martial arts teacher was standing behind me. A large grin broke across his face at my reaction and he let out a loud, hearty laugh, his eyes twinkling with amusement. "I didn't mean to startle you. I saw you watching the class through the window. My name's Mr. Hardy, I own the gym and martial arts school. You work out here, right?"

"Y-Yeah. It's very nice to meet you, Mr. Hardy. My name is Jeremy," I said as I tried to slow my heart rate to sub-marathon speed. I extended my hand to shake his. He clasped my hand and shook it with an iron grip. At that moment, I had an impulsive thought and I decided to act upon it. "Mr. Hardy, do you think I could sign up for martial arts classes?"

Mr. Hardy seemed taken aback at my forwardness. "Well, sure you could. What about working out in the gym? Would you want to do both or switch from one to the other?"

"As good as it is to do weights here, I would like to give martial arts classes a shot. What I saw today in your class was awesome, and I would like to see if I could get there at some point too." Mr. Hardy took this in and mulled it over for several seconds, never taking his eyes off me in the process.

"Alright. That sounds good, Jeremy. Let me get you the enrollment information so you can talk about it with your parents." He gestured for me to follow him into his office. As I followed him, I cast another look into the martial arts class. Even without the supervision of their headmaster, the class remained completely focused and tuned in to their drill. This display of self-discipline has stuck in my head to this day.

I stood in the doorway to Mr. Hardy's office as he collected several papers and put them into a manila folder. My eyes immediately started to wander across the walls, which were decorated extensively with weapons. Menacing butterfly knives were mounted next to several broadswords with ornate hilts. A personalized bo staff was centered over the desk. A pair of nunchakus was spread over a crossed pair of sais. Below the sais was a framed certificate detailing Mr. Hardy's induction into the Martial Arts Hall of Fame during the spring of 1992.

Mr. Hardy handed me the folder. "Let your parents know that they can call me if they have any questions or concerns. Have a good day, Jeremy! I'm looking forward to seeing you in the dojo soon."

"You too, Mr. Hardy!" I was having a hard time containing my excitement. This wasn't my first encounter with martial arts. I had taken classes when I was in elementary school for a short time, but the idea of joining Mr. Hardy's classes filled me with an excitement I had never felt before. The year 'The Karate Kid' came out in theaters, I started martial arts as an elementary-age child. Two years later, I stopped training. However, my interest in martial arts never faded, and seeing Mr. Hardy's class was what drove me to start my own journey in karate. I ran to my backpack, crammed the folder in, and ran out of the gym.

I was on my bike and pedaling for home before the door to Bodyworks closed behind me. I lived about a mile down the road, and my parents had recently allowed me to walk or ride my bike to the gym. As any other fourteen-year-old would, I was taking advantage of every ounce of freedom I could grab onto. Feeling the wind rush through my hair as I rode down the road further heightened my good mood. It was a beautiful spring day; a gentle wind, sunny skies and the hint of blossoms on the trees dancing in rhythm with the breeze.

I was turning into my driveway within minutes of leaving Bodyworks, as I had pedaled at breakneck speed. I got off my bike, half-leaned half-dropped it against the garage wall and leaped up the front steps three at a time. The spokes of the back wheel were still spinning as I threw the door open and stepped inside. Directly inside the front door was a mud porch that led into the kitchen area of the house. My father had taken time off his job to work on the house for the past few years, so there were tools and materials scattered here and there throughout the house, including the kitchen counters and island. "Mom, I'm home!" I shouted as I half walked out of, half tripped over my shoes on my way into the kitchen. My mother turned in surprise, her dark brown hair bouncing off her shoulders. She was in the middle of making tuna sandwiches, my favorite. "Hey, Mom! What are you having for lunch?" I asked, breaking into conversation.

"Uhm, the same as you. What's got you in such a good mood?" she said with a smile.

"I'd like to start doing karate at Bodyworks. I saw a karate class and I really want to do it!"

My mother seemed just as taken back as Mr. Hardy had been. "But you already work out up there. You can't do both with your schedule as it is," she pointed out, absently gesturing at me with a kitchen knife smeared with tuna.

"I've thought about that, and I'd be willing to switch from working out with weights to karate classes," I said with conviction. My mother knew how much I enjoyed the workout sessions. Seeing that I was so ready, almost anxious, to give up the gym for the dojo, my mother set the half-done sandwich on the counter and turned to face me. Her sharp gaze met and held mine, as if searching my expression for answers.

"Do you know about the schedule for karate classes? Or how much it will cost?" she asked. I answered her by opening my backpack and handing her the folder Mr. Hardy had given me. She smiled as she took it. "Jeremy, if you're anything, you're always prepared." I finished making the sandwiches as my mother examined the contents of the folder: a schedule of classes, the enrollment information, and a flyer detailing the school's martial arts program. I walked over to her with my sandwich in hand and peeked over her shoulder as she looked at the flyer. There were several pictures of classes in progress, students demonstrating different aspects of a class, and the instructing staff.

"You're sure this is something you want to commit to?"

"I'vf never been sururr off anyfing," I muttered through a large mouthful of sandwich. She looked at me for several seconds, then nodded her head and went back to scanning the contents of the folder. After discussing the program details with my father later that day, my parents gave me the go ahead to take up studying martial arts at Bodyworks Karate School. I was ecstatic, and took up the classes with a burning desire and eagerness to learn.

I dove right into the martial arts classes. I was so eager to learn everything and anything I could. Mr. Hardy jokingly called me a 'sponge' because of how quickly I would absorb information and be able to apply it. Classes were just as much of a workout as lifting weights, and I had a lot more fun doing them! But most importantly, I learned very early on in my training that if in a confrontation, one can usually settle the quarrel with minimal violence - and sometimes with no strikes at all. Mr. Hardy taught me that by taking someone down and executing either a wrist manipulation or other hold, it can take the fight right out of people. I certainly was in no mood to attempt to move after Mr. Hardy demonstrated the technique on me, so I knew that what he was teaching had plenty of merit.

One day in school, a few months after I had started training under Mr. Hardy, I was walking in the halls in between classes when I got shoved from behind. I already knew who it was; 'Harry', we'll call him. I turned around to glare at him. Even though he was about the same height as me, he was much larger in stature. I was muscular for an eighth grader, but he probably had forty pounds on me. He had a nasty sneer on his face which showed off his slightly yellowed teeth. "What's up, Sporto?" He proceeded to plow his shoulder through me, nearly knocking me into the lockers. I stared at his back as he walked down the hall without a backward glance. This treatment from Harry had become a regular occurrence. Whenever we were in the same hallway it was either a yank on the backpack strap that nearly floored me, or a smack on the back of the head. Harry always came out of nowhere. Even when I tried to avoid him, he'd still find some way to harass me. And it wasn't just me. Harry also did this to several other athletes in the school. While I wanted to confront him, two things held me back; my lack of self-confidence and my fear of getting in trouble with the school and my parents.

A few weeks later, my Dad and I were cleaning offices in Concord, part of a side business my Dad was running. The issue with

Harry had been on my mind a lot that day, as Harry had shoved me and knocked me into a girl that had just gotten to her locker. Her head smacked into the locker, but thankfully, she wasn't hurt. I was scrubbing a little more vigorously, doing everything a little more deliberately. I could tell my dad had noticed something was up, but he let me be the one to start the conversation. "Hey Dad, can I talk to you about something?" Without turning away from the desk he was cleaning, he mumbled, "mm-hmm." I proceeded to lay out the whole background regarding Harry at school, how I wanted so badly to give him a punch in the gut but also didn't want to get in trouble. After I was finished, my Dad answered me in a way that I'll never forget for as long as I live. He placed the cleaning supplies on the desk, turned to me, looked me in the eye and said:

"The next time Harry does something like that to you, you turn around and punch him right in the face." I was so taken aback by his answer. I was torn between total shock and rolling with laughter.

"Really, Dad?" I said through fits of laughter. "You're giving me permission to retaliate?" My dad answered with a stern nod of his head, no hint of humor or lightheartedness on his face. I was shocked, but pleased. I had my parent's permission to answer Harry's harassment at school.

I woke up the next day with a sense of relief. I headed into school not looking for trouble, but knowing that it would stop today. Sure enough, between third period and lunch, I felt a shove from behind followed by a "Move, moron!"

That was it. I'd had enough.

Without hesitating, I turned around and grabbed his right wrist with my left hand, his right shoulder with my right hand. I pulled his arm into my chest, lifted my right leg, and swept him down to the ground by throwing my right calf through his. The minute Harry was on the ground, I dropped my right knee into his ribs, knocking the wind out of him. I pulled up on his right arm to make it even more uncomfortable. People around us were yelling, but I didn't hear any of them. I was staring directly at Harry. His usual sneer was replaced by a look of surprise…and fear. His eyes were wide. They locked with mine. I put more weight on his ribs, making him wince. He tried to wriggle out from underneath me, but he wasn't getting anywhere: I had him pinned, all of my weight driving through my knee into his ribs. Finally, after a final push with my knee, I got up. I kept watching him as he scrambled to his feet. He dusted himself off and tried to save face. I turned on my heel and walked to the cafeteria, noticing that people were giving me a wide berth.

I learned a valuable lesson that day. Despite the fact that my father had given me permission to haul off on Harry, when the heat of the moment came, I didn't get into a fistfight. The only explanation I can think of is that I knew I didn't have to hit him. Just a short time into my martial arts training I had developed enough confidence to know I didn't need to punch him. In addition, I'm not sure that I could have stood toe-to-toe with Harry because of his size. Mr. Hardy was right; potentially violent situations could be resolved without violence. After that day Harry never gave me any trouble. There was no more pushing or shoving in the hallway. He would glare at me occasionally, but I wasn't worried. I had taken a stand. I had stood my ground. The boosts in self-confidence and self-discipline I had already gained from my short time training as a martial artist had proven to be well worth the effort.

Fast forward twenty years, and my interest in martial arts has only increased. My commitment to my training is still as strong as the day I joined. After studying any type of martial arts for an extended period of time (let alone two decades), it morphs from a hobby to a passion, and eventually to a lifestyle. Martial arts training means and represents something different for everyone that participates in it. If a group of ten black belts were surveyed, their definitions of how martial arts have influenced their lives would be ten different answers, unique for each individual.

Personally, my training started to affect my life right from the start. Within the first months, I had developed strong bonds with my classmates. As a group, we were all so different; at different points in our lives, with different degrees of income, having different reasons for starting martial arts, coming from different walks of life and having different likes and dislikes. Yet through all of the diversity, there was one common goal uniting us and bringing us together - the goal to better ourselves physically and mentally through training in the martial arts. Never, in any other type of gathering or organization, would as diverse a group come together and develop a connection as in a martial arts class. Several people who have met at Bodyworks have even gotten married!

The variety of individuals also helps in the learning process. While it's easy to toss someone around if you're bigger and stronger than they are, the application of correct mechanics is what it takes to effectively apply a technique in the martial arts. For example, muscling through a certain move or technique against someone smaller than you is something that doesn't require training and dedication to be able to perform. On the opposite end of the spectrum, applying a mechanically sound technique on someone who is a head-and-a-half taller and has thirty pounds on you, all while they are trying to resist requires practice, focus, and dedication to the training and the art. The more I work with different classmates, the more I learn about techniques that I've had for years. Sometimes I realize a more effective way to execute a move simply by working with a different classmate than I usually do. These classmates may also have different outlooks on a given move or technique that I had not considered. In the beginning of my training, I was not fond of working with people I was unfamiliar with. Now I relish it, both for the chance to learn more about my material and for the chance to learn more about my partner.

Martial arts and dedication are two concepts that go hand in hand. Similar to any hobby or passion, one must put in a significant amount of time, effort and commitment in order to become proficient. To become a successful football player, one must learn the plays, positions and strategies of football itself. Similarly, the basics, power principles and techniques of martial arts must be practiced and honed for years in order for one to truly become proficient. This idea of dedication is an excellent life lesson, especially for adolescents. A multitude of studies have shown that participating in martial arts increases the degree of etiquette, character, self-control, self-discipline, self-esteem and confidence in young children and teenagers. The idea that dedication and effort to a cause not only yields proficiency but that those efforts translate to overall positive growth as an individual is an invaluable lesson for kids and adults alike.

Rising through the ranks at Bodyworks has always been rewarding for me. While my main study is in the art of Combined Kenpo Karate, I have studied several other styles through Bodyworks. I earned my black sash in Mantis Kung Fu prior to earning my black belt in Kenpo. These two styles were taught separately at Bodyworks, as they are completely different. While Kenpo has its own set of principles, focuses and techniques, Kung Fu has a completely different look and feel. The Kung Fu style of movement is abstract and sporadic in comparison to Kenpo. Studying these systems simultaneously was challenging. While my knowledge base was growing rapidly, keeping both systems straight was difficult. I would sometimes confuse one form for another in the other system. Sometimes my instructors were able to relate concepts and principles from one system to the other. This was especially valuable for me as it taught me that lessons in one respect can be applied to other aspects of one's life.

Two of the more impactful milestones in my martial arts career were when I earned my black belts. As a young child, I dreamed about the idea of becoming a black belt one day. During every class at Bodyworks the goal of earning the rank of black belt was my motivation. Whenever I tested for a new rank, I knew I had moved one step closer to achieving my childhood goal. I would fall asleep thinking about the day I would be wearing that rank around my waist. The desire to become a black belt was like a drug.

I use the verb 'become' versus 'get' when referring to the rank of black belt for several reasons. First, an instructor by the name of Mr. Downing once told me several classes into my training when I was still a white belt, "That belt around your waist is a black belt. It just takes time to show through." This idea has stuck with me through my entire training; the idea that I can always do more than I think I can. Secondly, Mr. Hardy once posed a question to a karate class I was in. He asked, "How long does it take the average person to become a black belt?" The class was silent, pondering the question. After several seconds, one of my classmates slowly raised his hand.

"Uhm, ten years, sir?" Mr. Hardy smiled, surveying the class for other guesses.

"Eight years?"

"Six?"

"Twelve?"

Mr. Hardy stood in the front of the room, giving nothing away and allowing his students to work through the question. I had no clue as to what the answer could be. I had a feeling it wasn't a finite amount of time. Just as that thought crossed my mind, a hand to my left shot up in the air.

"The average person does not become a black belt, sir." Mr. Hardy beamed in response to the answer his student had just provided, going on to explain that if one puts forth the amount of dedication, perseverance and effort that is needed to become a black belt, they are anything but average. This is a message that has stuck with me throughout everything in my life. Whether one stops studying martial arts right after they earn their black belt or not, the lessons they have learned up to that point will forever stick with them, just as they have for me.

Mr. Jeff Hardy, Owner / Headmaster of Bodyworks Karate School

"One of my first memories of Jeremy was him coming into the school when we had a weightlifting area on one side of the school. He was there with several kids for a basketball conditioning program as a really young kid. He started training in martial arts shortly after that. Right from the start, Jeremy has had such an attention to detail with his training. Also, his level of respect for everyone, his instructors and students alike, is amazing. I know that with Jeremy, I'm always going to see an ultimate level of respect to instructors and fellow students."

"One memory that stands out to me of Jeremy is the process he went through for his black belt tests. During Jeremy's tests, he was one of only a handful of individuals who participated in two black belt tests at the same time. While testing for a black belt rank in Kenpo, he also tested for a black sash in Kung Fu. This meant that he would go from working tirelessly in one system to a completely different discipline with no break in between. To be able to move from one system to another in that fashion is unbelievable; no one else has gotten to the point Jeremy has with balancing these two systems. And he embodies the systems perfectly."

Every time I go in to train at Bodyworks I learn something new. Regardless of what is on the curriculum, no matter what mood I am in, there is always something new to learn, something to make more effective than last time, a different way to look at things. Such is the nature of martial arts. No one “perfects” a system, as that would take several lifetimes. Nowadays, more and more practitioners and schools are teaching more than one system at a time in a program. Bodyworks Karate School, for example, mainly teaches the art Combined Kenpo. However, Tai-Chi and Muay Thai Kickboxing classes are also offered. When I was starting out, Mantis Kung Fu was also offered as a program. Once the rank of black belt is achieved at Bodyworks in Kenpo, the system starts to add in elements of Northern Shaolin Kung Fu, Aikido and Brazilian Jiu Jitsu. With the melding together of all of these systems, there is literally no end to the learning process.

I’ve adapted that mindset to other areas of my life. I’ve found that by always striving to better myself and to continue learning, there’s always a goal to aim for. My training and experiences with martial arts have also taught me to focus on the minute aspects of life, to appreciate the small things, as they can make all the difference. An improper execution of a technique versus a successful application can come down to the tiniest detail, the smallest alteration in focus. I look at life the same way; rather than let myself be brought down by something, the smallest shift in outlook on my part can change the entire picture. The application of physical, mental and social concepts learned in my martial arts training have crossed into all aspects of my life. Since beginning my training in martial arts, I’ve developed a hunger for learning new things, as well as improving on practices that I already know. There’s not a karate class that goes by that I don’t learn something new. I strive to *always* learn something new, or learn how to go about something in a more efficient manner, in every day of my life.

Chapter Two
Transition Period

For most people, their high school years are ones filled with creating lifelong friendships, heartbreaks that seem like they'll never heal, and beginning to truly develop one's identity. These years for me were filled with the same elements. However, just like everyone else, my high school years had some unique events. This was a time in my life where I was forced to accept some difficult truths about life and learn some harsh lessons, but furthermore, I learned not to take any relationship for granted. Whether it was a friendship, family bond, girlfriend, teammate or classmate, I learned to cherish them all.

I grew up in Concord, New Hampshire, the state capital. It is a nice, homey city. With a distinct city district around the capital building and a rural, woodsy section in the northern part of town, Concord is a great place to live. There is always something fun and different to do in the city, and great nature walks in the northern part of Concord, along with the gorgeous Merrimack River carving through the center of the city. I went to Rundlett Middle school, which I attended from sixth to ninth grade. My class was large with roughly 400 kids in my grade. Even in middle school, I was a very active kid. Karate, basketball, and just being outside took up all of my free time.

When in school, I tended to zone out thinking about the previous night's karate class or what we would be drilling in basketball that day. Even more than most kids, I wasn't keen on reading textbooks. 'Study this, read that, memorize those' was what I constantly heard in school. I had no desire to be in class, at a desk, or in front of a textbook at home. I wanted to be in my gi and sparring with my classmates, learning a new offensive formation on the court with my friends and teammates. And with the large class sizes of twenty to thirty kids, it was easy to fly under the radar. When faced with the choice of drone on with twenty other kids in a geometry class or daydream about the many things I was looking forward to learning in karate and reliving the last basketball game where we crushed our rival team, it's pretty easy to guess which route I took.

Then came my sophomore year, tenth grade. I moved to Concord High School - the big campus. The large class sizes got even larger. My love for my extracurricular activities grew as my attention for classes dwindled. It's not that I was neglecting school, or that I was a bad kid. I just didn't want to be sitting still for hours on end when I could be on my feet. Halfway through the tenth grade, I came to the stark realization that I didn't really know how to study properly. For that matter, I wasn't really sure of how to be a good academic student at all. I knew with graduation and the real world looming just around the corner that I needed a solid foundation from high school. With the way I was going that foundation would be shaky…at best.

During my first semester in high school, I had a hard time adjusting. My grades were holding, but barely. I heard that basketball tryouts would be soon, which upped my spirits. I was determined to make varsity as a sophomore even though most sophomores never even get a chance at varsity. I practiced for tryouts every free moment that I had. In the days leading up to the tryouts I was completely confident that I had a spot all but locked up.

My performance in tryouts only worked to solidify that opinion. I gave it my absolute all and let everything on the floor. I did amazing, and thanks to a little bit of luck, everything fell into place during the drills and plays. As the tryouts winded down, the head coach started pulling kids aside one by one. I asked one of the older kids what was happening. He told me that the coach pulled you to the side and told you whether you made one of the teams or not. I could tell, because just as my potential teammate finished, the player that had been talking to the coach walked out of the gym with his head down.

The coach kept pulling kids aside as the rest of us played horse and around the world to pass the time until it was our turn to be pulled aside. I was one of the last to be called over. I followed the coach over to the side of the gym, the same area he had talked to everyone else. I knew I had performed that day, and was ready for great news.

"So, Jeremy, you did great today. You worked harder than anyone today and were one of the best on the court." I smiled, shifted my weight on my feet and nodded my head. It was good to hear that, and I was ready to hear more good news. "Even though you did just as good as any other person out there, I unfortunately can't give you a spot on the varsity team. I hate to say it, but as the coach, I have obligations to fill. However, you'll be my star on the JV team. You have the tools to shine on JV. Keep playing like you did today and you'll have a spot on varsity your junior year without question."

I was crushed. I was told I did as well as anyone else on the floor, but then had my hopes thrown down and stomped on. To be given those compliments only to have the rug pulled out from underneath me hurt. I wanted to scream in frustration. I had been thinking about varsity for weeks now, and to be told that I had the tools to be on varsity but not given a chance was harsh.

I lost focus in school following the news that I didn't land a spot on varsity. I didn't want to be in school. At the end of that week, I had an awful day and needed some alone time. I went for a walk from my house with no certain destination in mind. I just walked. I let my mind wander, zoning out my surroundings as my feet went on autopilot. As much as I tried to not focus on it, my thoughts kept circling back to the moment with the basketball coach. "You're definitely good enough, but I'm not going to put you on the team," is what I heard that day in the gym. He had sugarcoated it, but that's what he was really saying. After having time to reflect on the situation I felt that there were other reasons for the coach not putting me on varsity, making me even more resentful.

My walk took me to an empty parking lot. I found myself walking to the backside of a large, abandoned brick building. Before I knew it, I was choking up with a lump in my throat. I tried to fight them, but the tears weren't far behind. I let it out. I cried. I was so frustrated with that coach. I was so frustrated with school. My friends had noticed my demeanor change, and I had been snippy with them lately.

After crying all of my problems out, I composed myself through deep breaths and pacing back and forth. At that moment I made a promise that I have kept to this day; never again would I allow someone to do what that coach did to me. No one would ever again get me to that point of being so upset and discouraged.

Even though I knew that alone time in the parking lot had helped with my frustration and stress, I knew something had to change. It wasn't martial arts, karate had taught me to focus on what's important and to follow through on what mattered, like the studying that I despised. It wasn't basketball; all my friends were on the JV team, and that sport was my most important social connection in my life. That left one option: I needed to transfer schools. After my sophomore year ended, I did my research on what my options were. With my parent' guidance, I was able to connect with the right people at Bishop Brady, another high school in Concord. This would be a drastic change for me. Concord High was a public school with well over a thousand kids. Brady was a private Catholic school, with a student population of roughly 250 at any given time. In addition, all of my friends were at Concord High. I had grown up with those guys. But when it came down to it, I knew that I was trying to convince myself to stay at Concord High. Who was I kidding? I wasn't moving across the country, I could still see all of my buds on a regular basis.

My mind was made up. I talked to my parents and jumped through the many hoops required to set up my transfer to Bishop Brady High School. I attended Concord High for the first two weeks of my junior year. Then it was time. I said goodbye for now to my friends at Concord High, and started my time at Brady.

Immediately the smaller class sizes were a notable difference. Core classes that consisted of thirty students at Concord High were now only made up of six to ten students. This forced me to be more accountable for my schoolwork. After several weeks at Brady, basketball tryouts came around. I made the team and before I knew it I was settling in far better than I had hoped.

Not everything was a smooth transition, however. Shortly after transferring schools I came home to a not-so-nice surprise. A spiteful message had been left on our answering machine from one of my Concord High friends. He made physical threats against me if I were to ever go back to or visit Concord High. This came as a shock to me. This guy was my friend, or at least was supposed to be. The shock worsened when I kept getting these messages and even one or two threats in person when I was hanging out around town. These hurt even more because they were being made by my friends. Kids that I had grown up with were turning their backs on me left and right. Some made claims that I had transferred for a chance to be on a better basketball team. Overall, I quickly learned that people can be very cruel, and that people I had considered friends were not so friendly the minute something didn't go their way. I was forced to reexamine the people I had surrounded myself with. I had taken the first steps toward the first big change in my life and now I needed to shed the last bad remnant and surround myself with the right crowd.

This was, of course, easier said than done. Transferring schools was one thing. The slow but steady decrease in contact with my friends from Concord High was particularly hard for me to handle. I tried to stay in contact with my close-knit circle of friends from Concord High as much as I could. Before long, I only kept in touch with a small handful of friends from Concord High; all of my other close friends had faded into mere acquaintances. If we'd had social media back then, I can't imagine how much worse the taunting and bullying would have been. Going through the near hazing that came from switching schools caused me to grow a tough social exterior. I learned that as long as I was doing what was right for me, as long as I was making the right choices, as long as I was happy, everything would be fine. I learned that other people's opinions are just that: opinions.

After settling into the flow of Bishop Brady, I noticed my grades starting to improve. My study habits were getting better. My attention span for classes was lengthening. I was receiving individualized attention due to the smaller classes, which in turn made me into a more accountable student. Add in the basketball team at Brady and my continued study in the martial arts, and things were looking pretty great.

In my English class one day, a teammate from the basketball team invited me to a party. As with the vast majority of parties in high school, there was going to be alcohol there. It was a Friday and I didn't have anything going on the next day so I figured I'd take the plunge and attend my first high school party. I wasn't sure if I wanted to try alcohol or not, but the social scene was enticing. I mean, after only a few months of being at the school I was invited to a party. Of course I have to go, I rationalized to myself. Most of my new friends would be there so this would be a great opportunity to further cement myself socially in the school.

I went home, plowed through my homework for the weekend, and told my parents that I was heading over to a friend's house to have dinner with his family. I told them we would then head to the movies and head back to his place to spend the night. As I'd done this many times before and they knew my friend well, they had no objections and wished me a good night. I did head over to my friend's place but we had no intention of heading to the movies. My friend's parents were gone for the weekend so we didn't have any problem leaving his house to head to the party. The party was only a half mile from my friend's house, so we made it there in no time. From the road, it wasn't obvious that there was a party. There wasn't any loud music blaring, no cars parked along the road and there wasn't a light show happening at the house. Regardless, I was extremely paranoid as I walked up to the house, constantly looking over my shoulder as if some random passerby would see me walking up to the house and know my whole situation and scream for the police.

Once inside, it was totally different. There was probably forty kids in the house. Almost everyone had either a beer bottle or a plastic cup in their hand. Some people had obviously had their fair share of alcohol, as they were teetering in place. We had arrived at the party at ten even though the invite had said eight. Music was flowing through the house; I could feel the bass reverberate slightly through my body. Some of the faces I knew right away, others looked familiar, and still more were foreign to me. My friend and I made our way from the front door through the crowd and found my teammate who was hosting the party, having a drinking contest in the kitchen. After downing a beer he made eye contact, wiped his mouth with his sleeve, welcomed me with a rough hug and asked if I wanted a drink. I hesitated before sheepishly declining. He pointed to where the alcohol was and invited me to help myself at any point in the night, then headed to the door to welcome someone else to the party.

I was left in front of the alcohol, alone. People were mingling all around me, all slightly bobbing to the music. As for me, I was still looking at the vast array of booze strewn across the countertop. There were several cases of beer scattered between bottles of light and dark liquor, along with bottles of soda and juice. I didn't know the first thing about what went well as far as mixers and liquor, so I quickly ruled those out. 'Well, what the hell…when in Rome…' I thought to myself, and grabbed a beer bottle.

Half an hour passed and I was still sipping at that first beer. I hated the taste. It tasted like expired seltzer water mixed with coffee grinds, but I didn't want to look like a chump and not finish it. I was talking to two of the people that had first befriended me at Brady. One seemed pretty buzzed; she was draining her drink really fast while giggling at everything. The other was downright trashed: he was stumbling around and couldn't focus on anything. Suddenly, I heard a *crash* from behind me.

I turned around to see a large group of people parting into a semicircle with two guys in the middle. For this story, we'll call these two Flannel and Thunder. Flannel was a scrawny kid, about five and a half feet tall, and maybe 120 pounds and wearing a red and black flannel shirt. Thunder, on the other hand, was a football player, and was almost six feet and pushing 200 pounds. Apparently, the crashing sound had been Thunder (who was belligerently drunk) stumbling into Flannel and knocking him into the counter, which had knocked Flannel's beer everywhere based on the fresh wet stain all over his shirt. Flannel, who was also fairly tipsy, shouted, "What the hell, man? Watch yourself."

Thunder didn't appreciate this too much and got in Flannel's face.

"And if I don't? What are you going to do?" said Thunder with a sneer. Flannel didn't hesitate in answering by stiff-arming Thunder back, prompting 'Ooooo!'s from the onlookers. 'Bad move, Flannel,' I thought to myself. Sure enough, Thunder hauled off and threw a haymaker at Flannel, knocking him to the ground. Thunder followed him down and got one more punch off before Thunder's friends pulled him up to his feet and backed him off. Several of Flannel's friends rushed in to help. I was able to catch a glimpse of Flannel's face as they stood him up; his temple was split open, his left eye was already starting to swell and his cheek had a split in it. Blood was oozing out of the split on his temple, with a little dripping to the floor as his friends walked him out the front door and left the party.

I was shaken up. Even though neither of the two were friends of mine, I knew enough about them to know that neither would have acted as they just did under normal circumstances. Flannel was a fairly shy kid, and Thunder was pretty hard to rile up and usually quite polite. Seeing firsthand what alcohol could lead people to do was very scary. Disgusted, I tossed my half-finished beer into the trash, found my friend, and told him I was heading back to his place and would see him in the morning.

Alone on the walk back, I had plenty of time to think about what I had just witnessed. It hadn't taken much to spark the dispute, and it was over almost as quickly as it had started. What if I had been on either end of a conflict like that at a party after drinking heavily? What if I lost control and hurt someone? What if someone, under the influence of alcohol or drugs, tried to start something with me at a party? With the training I've had in martial arts, I could really hurt someone if I went at them without check. Seeing what I had and thinking these thoughts troubled me. I needed to talk to someone, an authority figure.

I couldn't talk to my parents. "Hey Mom, Dad, I'm not even

eighteen and I went to a party and drank but want to talk about something else that happened." Yeah, that would go over real well. Maybe a teacher at school? No, then they'd have to talk to administration and more meetings and retelling my story over and over. Then I thought of the answer: Mr. Hardy, my martial arts instructor. I could talk to him about this. I held him in the highest regard, and I valued his opinion.

The next day at karate, I approached Mr. Hardy after class and asked him if he had a few minutes to spare. He nodded and invited me into his office. He closed the door, sat down in his chair and gestured to an adjacent chair for me. "So what's on your mind, Jeremy?" Mr. Hardy asked with a smile. I took a moment, thought about how to start the conversation, and tentatively began retelling the events of the previous night. I explained my curiosity to see what alcohol was like, as well as my initial hesitation when actually presented with the opportunity. I assured him I had only consumed half of a beer. I told him about the one-sided conflict that had happened out of nowhere. I finished with my concerns after having had time to think about what I had witnessed at the fight. "I was thinking about someone I could talk to about this, and you seemed like the best person, sir," I said as I leaned back in the chair, anxiously awaiting his response. He remained still for several moments, staring off just past my shoulder at the wall. As he was running his hand through his goatee I noticed that the smile had left his face, and in its place was a look of concern and seriousness.

"Well, Jeremy, I appreciate you coming to me. I'm glad you feel that you can come to me, as you should. My door is always open, regardless of the situation. Now, you're right to be worried about what would happen if you got in a fight. You've been training here, between the gym and martial arts, for two years now, and have been taught some excellent self-defense techniques. It is *critical* to remember that these techniques are taught with the intent that they only be used in a defensive manner, only to be used if provoked. Our student creed says specifically, 'I intend to use what I learn in class constructively and defensively, to help myself and others, and never to be abusive or offensive."

"Becoming a part of this party scene would go against everything you state in the creed. You could end up using your training in an offensive and destructive manner, you would certainly not be helping yourself or others and you'd be abusing substances that are illegal at your age." This struck a chord with me. I agreed that abusing drugs or alcohol was a violation of the creed, the promise of a martial artist. "Jeremy, I am glad that you tossed that beer out and left the party. That was the best decision you made last night. But the worst was attending the party in the first place. As a martial artist, you should hold yourself to a higher social standard. Just because you don't physically train martial arts in school or in public doesn't mean you stop being a martial artist. The martial artist lifestyle is one of etiquette, self-control and self-discipline. Going to that party was a disregard for all of those."

"Let me make one thing clear, Jeremy. I hope that this experience you've had has convinced you beyond a shadow of a doubt to NOT become a member of that crowd. If I find out that you are abusing drugs or alcohol, you will no longer be a student in this school. I know that neither of us wants it to come to that, but only one of us can assure that never has to be a situation we face. Make the right choices, Jeremy. You have great things going for you and you're an excellent student with a bright future. Don't throw all of that away." He finished his talk and allowed me to process for several seconds. Those seconds felt like forever. My headmaster had just given me an ultimatum. Avoid partying or lose my home away from home. Even though I wasn't fond of the party scene at all, especially after the previous night, I was shocked that he had been that sharp about it. The thought of losing Bodyworks scared me. I felt that I belonged here, that it was part of my identity. I assured

Mr. Hardy that I would avoid that scene like the plague, that I valued Bodyworks too much to gamble it like that. "Good!" exclaimed Mr. Hardy, his illuminating smile reappearing. "I'm glad it means that much to you. Well thank you for coming to me with this, Jeremy. Keep up the good work in class, and make good decisions!" We shook hands, I wished him a good rest of the evening and headed home.

I will never forget that talk. To this day, I look at Bodyworks as a second home, and the people there as family. That heart-to-heart I had with Mr. Hardy ensured that I would stay on the right path through high school. That party was the one bump in an otherwise excellent journey through my high school career at Bishop Brady. To top it off was an equally great end to my basketball career.

In high school, I wasn't a big scorer - or the ace on the team. But when I did play, I gave it my all and helped my team through some hard-fought games. During my senior year, we made it to the state championship game for our division. This was the first time that I had been involved in a state championship game, so I was a bundle of nerves mixed with a boatload of excitement. My school, Bishop Brady, would be playing Goffstown High School for the championship. We had such talent on our team, especially for a school of our size. In a school of about 250 kids total, our team's starting five players consisted of two "D1" level players and three "D2" players, an incredible arsenal.

Game day came around, and I was anxious to get out on the court and put an exclamation point on the end of my high school years. My team was gathered in the locker room by our amazing coach, Mr. Frank Monahan, and he gave us an excellent speech that instilled confidence and pride. We then moved to just outside of the gymnasium doors. Just before we were about to enter the gym one of the starters came up to me, holding the game ball. He handed to me and said, "We want you to lead us out, Jeremy." I was shocked. I had never led the team out. Ever. And this was the biggest game in any of our high school careers.

"Really? Seriously?" He chuckled and tapped the basketball twice, then put his arm around my shoulder and walked me to the front of the line. The sense of camaraderie I remember feeling in that moment is indescribable. My chest was swelling with pride. As I got to the front of the line, I heard our team announced over the P.A. system. That was my cue to start leading the team out. With only the slightest bit of hesitation, I jogged out onto the court, dribbling the game ball, thinking about how amazing it was that my parents were seeing me lead my team out for our championship game in front of a packed house of 2,500 spectators.

The idea behind leading a team out is to dribble to the hoop, toss in an easy lay-up and pass the ball to the teammate behind you, who will repeat the process. Once you've made the lay-up and passed the ball, you move to half-court and line up. A simple process, especially for a senior. Regardless, my head was suddenly filled with thoughts or tripping over my own feet or dribbling the ball off my foot and losing it. I was praying that none of these things would happen. Fortunately, nothing like that happened. Unfortunately, something worse did.

My foot came down on the three-point line and I started executing the lay-up. It was my go-to layup, one that I had been doing since I was in elementary school. I focused in on the basket, lifted one leg slightly off the ground, brought the ball higher, and took the shot.

I missed. Badly.

The ball ricocheted off the rim and nearly bounced off my head. I backtracked, sheepishly grabbed the ball and tossed it back to my teammate. I jogged to half-court as fast as I could. With my hands clasped behind my back, I started a hole in the gym wall ahead of me. 'I blew it, I blew it, I blew it, what the hell, how did I blow it? The ONE time I absolutely needed to hit an easy shot,' I thought. My thoughts were cut short as the junior starter that had handed me the game ball trotted next to me and gave me a clap on the back. "Nice shot, Jeremy. I'm sure the scouts in the crowd are drooling over you after that!" I couldn't help laughing along with him. Several more of my teammates came up to me in line and joked with me about the shot. Even though I had goofed, we had a championship game to win, and nothing could dampen my mood at this point.

Goffstown came out, did their lay-ups and lined up across from us. After the pre-game formalities, it was game on! It was a fast-paced game. Goffstown was good, very good. At halftime it was a close game, with Brady up by seven. Coach huddled us up and gave us pointers on what we needed to keep doing and what we needed to change. The second half was quite different from the first.

We really started to pull away from Goffstown. We were hitting clutch shot after clutch shot. We made great defensive plays and would answer immediately with quick baskets. There was one particular play where I danced around a Goffstown defender, pulled off some great footwork and drained a lay-up. I found my parents in the audience and flashed them a smile while pointing to them.

Marshall Crane, basketball teammate / longtime friend

"Jeremy was never the ace on our basketball team, but he also wasn't a bench warmer. He always had a love and passion for the game of basketball and camaraderie with his teammates. Whether he was playing in a game or he was on the sidelines, he was almost as vocal as the coach in the games, always supporting our entire team. He wasn't going to be recruited by schools for basketball, but man, he gave EVERYTHING when he was on the court. Since high school, I've played with players that have gone on to get seven figure salaries professionally, and Jeremy is still my favorite teammate I ever had. He and his brother

Jamie were excellent on the team. Even to this day, he still displays that same level of passion that I first saw on the basketball court."

We went on to win the game by a score of 77-51. Bishop Brady was the 1997 Division Champion! I was ecstatic. I was so psyched that I wasn't even on cloud nine; I was looking down on cloud nine. We had played an amazing game against an amazing opponent. We had been coached through an amazing season by an amazing coach. My last basketball season was perfect, I couldn't have asked for more. That championship game was certainly the exclamation point I was hoping it would be.

Chapter Three
The College of Real Life

The rest of my senior year flew by, and I graduated from Bishop Brady in much better academic standing than I had hoped for. I was anxious about leaving high school, but excited at the same time for the opportunities that lay ahead of me. I knew I wanted to go to college, but I didn't want to relocate; all of my family was local, and I was rooted in my martial arts training at Bodyworks too much to give it up. I started looking at local colleges. I was interested in a physical fitness or sports science degree. All of the big four-year colleges on the local level only offered concentrations in these areas, not a full degree program. Also, the tuition rates were staggering. Coupling this with a lack of financial aid options available to me, I turned down the idea of pursuing a bachelor's degree. I decided I would stay on the lookout for college programs while I continued to work the retail position I'd had since the ninth grade.

I had started working in retail my freshman year of high school. I'm glad that I started working early for a number of reasons. First, it made the transition into 'the real world' that much easier, as I'd already gotten a taste of it through work. It allowed me to start getting a feel for the financial side of life; getting paychecks and managing money instead of tossing it anyway the first chance I got. Not having to depend on my parents for money if I wanted to head out with friends for a night of fun was an upside too. Second, it taught me social skills that I couldn't learn anywhere else. Whether it was working a register, assisting customers or stocking shelves and doing inventory, working in retail taught me that even in a straightforward and simple business, there are many positions and responsibilities that need to be addressed. I could never have learned all of this from a textbook, or from sitting in a chair taking notes.

Halfway through the summer of 1997, I was neck-deep in my college search. I was looking through two-year tech schools in the area. I looked into NHTI (New Hampshire Technical Institute) and what programs they offered. They had two programs that interested me: an exercise science program and a small business program. After more research into the class schedules, tuition rates and the contents of the programs themselves, I decided to apply.

I was accepted into the exercise science program and enrolled in the fall semester. My first day of college was just as exciting to me as the first day of high school. I had been familiarizing myself with the campus throughout the summer. My first class was an introductory exercise science class. The course, the professor and my fellow students were all great; it was certainly a good start to college that had me optimistic about the rest of my program. For my first assignment, I had to write an essay discussing where I saw myself in the future. I focused on three different time frames: one year, five years and ten years in the future. In one year, I intended to be continuing my education at the institute, building the foundation for a career. In five years, I hoped to be a physical fitness trainer in some capacity. As for the long-term outlook, my dream was (and still is) to own a chain of fitness gyms.

While this essay was the cliché 'intro to college' essay, it was very useful for me. It allowed me to lay out my plans, thoughts, hopes and dreams for the future. It formed a timeline for my path into a career in the physical fitness field. I didn't know where or how I would be a trainer, but I knew I would. I didn't know where or how I would open a gym, but again, I knew I would. I'd always been one to aim high and set goals. Now I just needed to make it happen.

My business class didn't turn out so well. My accounting professor was interesting and he was a good teacher, so it was nothing against him. He worked hard to make the class fun, but there were no hands on experiences or lessons whatsoever. At the end of my first semester, I looked at what I had learned so far in college. I had learned a lot from my exercise science class that I would be able to put to good use. I learned a few things from my accounting class regarding a small business as well. However, the college experience wasn't what I had expected. I didn't want to be there, and I even started dreading my exercise science class. A good majority of the kids in my classes were very immature, with next to no motivation for any of the class discussions or topics. Because of this, I had a hard time focusing on discussions in class and on work outside of it. I decided that one semester was enough for now; I wanted to get into the 'real world' and start putting my life together. My parents and grandparents all owned businesses, and I wanted to get that hands-on experience I was craving.

For the next two years I split my time between retail and the family business. This kept me busy, which was exactly what I wanted. I loved always having something on my schedule, I couldn't (and still can't) just sit around. On average I was working about sixty hours a week, which left just enough time for a social outing here and there. During this time, I was poking my head around and seeking out potential physical trainer positions. Unfortunately, a vacant position was nowhere to be found. But I was determined. I didn't let a dead end get me down. I bided my time, kept working and building up my people skills, and continued to look for trainer positions.

In the spring of 2000, something odd occurred. One day while helping my Dad clean offices, I noticed that some of my joints were black and blue all around them, as if I had been beaten. There were more spots like this the next day, and more the day after that. I was worried. I knew that they weren't from my martial arts classes. I decided to give it another day, and if it got worse I would go to the doctors.

The next day, I woke up feeling like I had been hit by a train. My parents noticed that something was off as I was heading out for work that morning. Mom said that I looked pale and abandoned her cereal to pull me under the light in the kitchen. From the table, Dad watched over the top of his newspaper, large glasses peering out over the headlines. "Honey, you're burning up, sweating, and you look awful!" she said as she clutched my cheeks. I could see the concern and worry in her eyes but it didn't register. I shrugged my mother's worry off and took some medicine to placate her and told her I'd be fine. Luckily, the spring weather was particularly chilly that day: I was wearing a sweatshirt and pants, concealing the black and blue marks that surely would have had my mom up in arms.

I half-walked, half-fell out of the house and left for work. I remember bits and pieces of the rest of the day. One minute I was pulling out of the driveway, the next minute I'd be five miles down the road with no recollection of the driving in between. I was spacing out. It started to get scary. But I was already more than halfway to the mall where I worked, so I figured I'd just keep going. I was constantly wiping sweat from my brow in between chills that shot through my entire body. My eyelids were heavy, I just wanted to close my eyes and feel better...*BANG!* from behind. The car was rocked forward and the front bumper slammed into the pavement. I was disoriented, looking around and trying to figure out what had happened. I turned around to see that the driver behind me was backing up slowly from rear-ending me, their front bumper dragging against the pavement on one side. 'Great, my first accident. This is just what I need,' I thought as I pulled my car over to the side of the road.

Once I pulled over and out of the path of traffic, I shut off the engine and let the keys fall to the floor. I slumped over with my forehead on the steering wheel and let out a huge exasperated breath. The cool feel of the steering wheel felt good against my forehead, which was still sweaty. I don't know how long I sat like that. It might have been a few seconds or it might have been five minutes. A sharp rap against my window jolted me upright. I looked out to see two men looking at me. "Are you okay, man?" the taller of the two asked. I nodded in response, and they backed up so I could open up my door.

Opening the door took more effort than it should have, as did getting out of the car. It took a moment for my vision to clear. The two men, dressed in baggy shirts, ripped pants and backwards baseball caps were staring at me. "Man, I'm sorry that it shook you up so bad. You look rough, want a smoke?" the taller one said as he pulled out a cigarette and lit it. I didn't acknowledge his question as I walked to the back of my car to assess the damage. The short walk made me light-headed. The honk of a car horn cut through the air and made me jump, and made my head pound harder. I winced at the waves of discomfort shooting through me.

The back of my car was pretty banged up. The bumper was hanging by a thread. When I went to try and pick up the detached end, the entire thing came off and clattered to the ground. I disregarded the bumper and looked at the rest of the damage. My driver's side lights were completely hanging out of the car, dangling in place only by their wires. I tried to prop them back in but they fell right back out. I pushed harder, but got the same result. The third attempt, I smashed them into place with a grunt of effort. Yet again, the pounding took over my skull and I fell to the ground. The two men ran to me asking what was wrong. I shrugged them off and got up to put the bumper in the trunk, only to discover that the trunk wouldn't open because the latch was bent in.

"Yo, sir. You gonna say something, or keep ignoring us? We're just trying to make sure you're okay."

"I'm fine," I muttered as I got to my feet, holding my bumper in a bear hug. I walked past the two men and opened the car door. I shoved the bumper into the back seat, leaned against the door frame and looked at the men. Their worried looks were gone. They now looked scared. The smaller man pulled out his phone and said he was calling the cops to sort things out. "No, don't worry about it. It's all good. I have to get to work," I said. My words were starting to slur. I just wanted to get to work.

"Are you drunk, man? It's kinda early for that." The men looked irritated. "Look, we know this was our fault, we just want to get it sorted out."

"Forget it, man. I have to get going."

"You're going to leave the scene of an accident? We haven't even exchanged insurance information, dude!" I didn't care at that point. I was already late for work, and I felt terrible. I ignored the men, got in my car and drove off. Luckily, I was less than five minutes from work. After a terrible parking job, stumbling through the doors to the mall and receiving countless glances from workers opening their stores, I walked toward Abercrombie and Fitch for work.

Surprisingly I was only fifteen minutes late to work. I had called the store as I was leaving the accident scene to let them know I'd be late. Before going into the store, I had stopped by the bathroom and tried to pull myself together. A face full of cold water helped a little bit. After drying off my face and taking several deep breaths I headed into Abercrombie and Fitch. I walked into an empty store, as the mall itself had just opened for the day. Ryan, my coworker that had answered the phone was waiting for me in front of the register. "Hey Jeremy, are you okay? You look pretty rattled." I told him that it was just a busted bumper and a few other scrapes. He asked if I had called anyone to the scene. 'No,' I responded as casually as I could. "Why not? Now it's going to be a hassle to get your car fixed," Ryan said.

"Eh, I'll figure it out. I'm going to head out to the stockroom and get some stuff squared away back there, let me know if you need help on the floor or at the registers." Without waiting for a response, I made my way to the back.

"Jeremy, are you sure you're okay to work?" I held up a thumbs-up in response as I opened the door to the stockroom. I could feel his stare burning into my back - almost as hot as the burning I was feeling from a particularly bad hot flash. The sound of the door shutting rang through my skull and caused me to grimace. I turned off half of the lights in the room so I didn't have to squint. There were four of us working the afternoon shift. The other three were all out on the floor and at the registers so I had the stockroom to myself. I looked around the room for a chair so that I could rest. I spotted several metal fold-out chairs sitting against a large stack of boxes. I grabbed the top chair and carried it over to the fan. My bad luck continued. The electrical plug was bent out of alignment, so I had to force it straight to fit into the socket, a project in the state I was in. I was dripping sweat again, so I removed my sweatshirt and draped it over the back of the chair. I turned the fan on and sat down, sighing heavily.

Within ten minutes, I was chilled to the core. Even putting my sweatshirt back on and turning the fan off did not stop my shivers. Looking back, I remember being very scared in that moment. I had no idea what was wrong with me. I rolled up my sleeve and looked at my elbow. It was a mess of blotchy black-and-blue coloring. I promised myself that I would go to the hospital after my shift.

I stayed in the stockroom for hours. I couldn't bring myself to go out on the floor. All my coworkers came in to check on me and offered their support. When I found some energy here and there, I did manage to get some work done moving new stock to where it needed to be and doing inventory. After what felt like an eternity, my shift was over. On the way out, Ryan offered to follow me to the hospital, 'just in case'. With the accident that had occurred this morning, I was happy for any help I could get. Luckily, the 45-minute ride up to Concord Hospital was uneventful. Ryan wished me luck and asked me to keep him informed. I agreed to do so and waved goodbye before turning and walking to the hospital doors. While I was nervous about the possibilities, I was ready to figure out what was plaguing me.

After checking in and describing my symptoms, I was directed to urgent care. This, of course, did nothing to calm my nerves. I had barely been sitting in the waiting room for a minute when my name was called. I forced myself out of the chair and made my way through the door being held open by the friendly-looking doc. Odd paintings lined the walls down to the exam rooms. A painting of blue flowers in a purple vase sat across the hall from another that was just scattered lines and haphazardly strewn colors. The doctor pulled my thoughts away from the paintings by directing me to a room with an open door. I hobbled in and clumsily shuffled up onto the exam table.

"Okay. Jeremy Woodward, is it?" I nodded my head. "Well Jeremy, what seems to be the problem?" I proceeded to describe my symptoms and to show him the marks on my joints. He asked how long I'd been experiencing these and how severe the symptoms were, jotting down notes furiously the whole time. He had me rate my pain and discomfort on a scale of one to ten, saying one is minimal and ten is excruciating. I chose eight, since the fatigue and other things I was experiencing were alarming, particularly that my symptoms fluctuated so much. Finally, he said that he had one last question and asked when the last time was that I had eaten and what it was I had. I told him that I hadn't even had breakfast that day because of how crummy I felt.

After I had answered all of his questions, he flipped through some papers for a few seconds. The doctor then put his papers down and looked at me. "Jeremy, I would like to do what is called a 'TEE' scan." He explained to me that this stood for Trans-Esophageal Echocardiogram, and that the purpose was to take a thorough set of pictures of my heart and the major blood vessels. Even though I asked the doctor in five different ways for specifics on what he thought my problem could be, all he would say was something to the effect of, "it could be a heart-related condition, but we'll need the TEE scan to be sure."

I was given time to call my parents while the medical staff prepared a room for the procedure. That was a hard call to make. I decided to call my father and explain my situation to him and allow him to tell my Mom, since I knew I couldn't handle hearing Mom's reaction. I told him what was going on, where I was and where the medical staff had told me they could wait for the test results. "Dad, I'm nervous. What if they find something terribly wrong?"

"Then it's a good thing that you're in the best place to be when things are wrong." I had to hand it to him, my Dad had the most level head of anyone I knew. "We'll be there in fifteen minutes, son. Will you be in the scan room by then?" I passed the question on to a nurse, who said yes. "Then we'll see you when you're out. Stay strong pal."

Knowing that my parents would be here made this whole process a lot more bearable. The worst I'd ever had was a broken arm; now I was about to be put under and have a tube put down my throat to find out what possible heart condition I had! Luckily I wasn't left alone with my thoughts. The nurse that had answered the question for my Dad had been waiting until I finished my phone call to guide me into the operating room.

I tried not to let my mind wander. In fact, I tried to focus on absolutely nothing. But when I saw the entire cardiac lab, I couldn't help but look around and take everything in. The first thing I noticed was a massive machine that resembled a vice grip positioned above the operating table. It was attached to several mounts and levers that were attached to the ceiling. I guessed that it could be moved and controlled from the small computer mounted in front of it. Next to the vice grip were several gray sections of tubing that ran from the arm of the vice grip into the ceiling. One section of this tubing bunched together near a white metal arm that supported a large array of computer or television screens. There were four separate screens, all of them blank. Beyond that, there were several more monitors, control panels and sets of small tools dispersed throughout the room.

There was a different doctor in the lab than the one that had initially evaluated me. He introduced himself and the nurse that would be assisting him. He then went on to explain exactly what would be happening. I would be receiving a light sedative for my mouth, and they would then be inserting a long, thin tube down my throat to monitor and take pictures of my heart. While I wasn't thrilled that there would be a tube hanging out in my throat, the knowledge that it should only take twenty minutes and I wouldn't be able to feel it made me feel a little bit better. And overall, I just wanted answers regarding the mystery illness that had been plaguing me.

The preparation for the procedure took longer than I expected. The doctor and nurse had to check all the tools, suit up and get me situated. After a few minutes, the nurse was spraying a sedative into my mouth. I expected a nasty flavor or taste, but there was none. Within ten seconds I could barely feel any of the pokes or prods she was doing to test my sensitivity. She helped me move onto my left side, adjusting my angle until she deemed it fit. The doctor then walked around the table and stood over me. "Okay, here we go, Jeremy. If at any point you feel uncomfortable or need a break, just let me know with a tap on the leg. Are you ready?" I nodded yes, laid back and opened my mouth. He tilted my head for a better angle, and the procedure started.

It was a lot less uncomfortable than I had expected. While I wouldn't say it was fun, the sedatives made it nearly painless. The monitors were on the opposite side of the table, so I wasn't able to see what the doctor was viewing. Twenty minutes later, the tube was removed and I was told I sat still like a champ.

"So from here, I'm going to review the recordings once or twice. I'll call you back in to go over the results. You can have your parents with you or not when we go over the scan, that's your call. Until then you can head out into the waiting area with your parents," the doctor said with a comforting smile. I shook his hand and walked out of the lab. I ended up walking past the same paintings as before on my way back from the lab. I tried to make sense of the seemingly random lines and colors in the abstract painting, but to no avail. The painting looked like I felt; strewn all about and without any sense.

The minute I opened the door to the waiting room, my mother ran up and hugged me. "Oh honey! Are you okay? How are you feeling? What happened to your car? What did they say?!"

"Hun, keep your voice down and give him some breathing room," my dad said, guiding me over to a seat. I sat down and told them everything that had happened from that morning up until the procedure. While my parents were upset at how I had handled the accident in the morning, they gave me the benefit of the doubt due to my condition. Then I filled them in on what the doctor had told me to that point. My parents offered words of support and phrases such as 'everything will be okay' to try and keep my spirits up. We made small talk to pass the time, talking about how our days went and what we would have for dinner that morning, they gave me the benefit of the doubt due to my condition. Then I filled them in on what the doctor had told me to that point. My parents offered words of support and phrases such as 'everything will be okay' to try and keep my spirits up. We made small talk to pass the time, talking about how our days went and what we would have for dinner that night. About a half hour passed by before the doctor who had operated on me came out to the waiting area and called me back in to discuss the scan. I muscled myself up and motioned for my parents to follow me in to the cardiac lab.

We all filed into the lab and sat in the three seats that the doctor had lined up next to the examination table. Once we were all seated and he had introduced himself to my parents, he started.

"Okay, so as you know, I performed a TEE scan on Jeremy, who was an excellent patient by the way. The purpose of the TEE scan was to check for any abnormalities related to the heart. Jeremy's symptoms pointed to a potential heart condition and the easiest way to know one way or the other is through a TEE scan." He then pulled up still images on the screens. "Now right here is an image of one of your valves, Jeremy, the aortic valve to be exact. This here is a still image of yours. One moment…" He fiddled with a remote and pulled up a second image on the adjacent screen. "And here's what a normal aortic valve looks like." I looked back and forth between the two pictures and could see that there looked to be a fissure and bubbly surface on mine. This was a truly terrifying moment. I had so many questions but at the same time I didn't want to ask any, so I simply sat in silence. I had a terrible sinking feeling in my stomach.

"As you can see, this area of your aortic valve looks distorted in comparison to the other picture. From what I'm seeing here, that indicates that you have a severely deteriorated and slightly inflamed area on your valve. This is a condition known as endocarditis. It can be brought on by bacteria that enter the blood stream and settle on the heart valve, which is what I suspect happened here. This can happen in any number of common and everyday manners."

"Wh, what? Endocarditis?!" My mom gasped, shooting her hand to her mouth. "But how? How on earth?"

"Doctor, what does this mean for the immediate future? We know what is wrong, now what are the potential solutions?" My dad turned to me and mouthed, 'what?' with a furrowed brow. Dad had asked the question that I was afraid to ask. I was even more afraid to hear the answer.

"Sir, your son requires open-heart surgery to repair his valve. As soon as possible."

Chapter Four
Under the Knife

Those words hit me harder than any strike I'd ever received in karate. Open heart surgery. I felt my jaw go slack. One of my parents put their hand on my shoulder. The rest of the room faded out of view except for the two images on the screens. I think my mother hugged my father and was gasping, or crying, I'm not sure. I was really afraid. Having the TEE scan had made me nervous enough, now I had to undergo open-heart surgery?! What about time off from work? What about the cost of the surgery? What about the risks? Side effects? Future changes for me physically? All of these thoughts were crashing through my brain. I could barely focus before another horrible thought barreled through my brain. I went on an entire emotional roller coaster of dread in that moment. The doctor was saying something, but I was still tuned out. His muffled voice was at the edge of my thoughts. I tried to focus in and hear what he was saying, but I couldn't. My father shook my shoulder, snapping me back into the present. I looked back at him and he gestured to the doctor.

"Sorry, I zoned out."

"Don't apologize. Situations such as this that pop up seemingly out of nowhere are often hard to grasp. I wish there was an easier way to deliver news like this. The good news is that by treating it now, you'll be fine afterwards. You'll have to have check-ups and echoes here and there, but you'll be absolutely fine." From there, the doctor explained the best course of action. I was going to stay overnight for monitoring at Concord Hospital.

The next day I would be driven down to Boston. Monitoring the surgery itself and recovery, according to the doc, would take about a week. There was also the choice of replacing my valve with a tissue valve or a mechanical valve.

There were pros and cons to both. A tissue valve wouldn't require nearly as much maintenance and upkeep as a mechanical valve. However, I would need another surgery in roughly ten to fifteen years, as tissue valves will deteriorate over time.

On the other hand, mechanical valves regularly lasted for thirty or more years before needing surgical maintenance. With a mechanical valve, I would have to take Coumadin daily for the rest of my life in order to prevent blood clotting. My parents and I talked the options over for what felt like an eternity. We decided on going with a tissue valve. I thought to myself, 'I will prove these doctors wrong. Ten to fifteen years? I was a strong 20-something year old, I'd make that tissue valve last double the time they were telling me!'

After my parents asked the doctor several more questions, I walked with them out to the waiting room. They were going to go home and pack some things for me while I was in Boston. They would be able to be in Boston for most of the process, but I knew they both couldn't take too much time off from work. I let them know what I wanted from home, hugged them both and watched them walk out the rotating doors to the car.

The same friendly nurse guided me up to the counter and had me fill out a little bit of extra paperwork before showing me to a room. From what I understood, I'd be in here until morning. We went in an elevator, out of the urgent care building and into another massive brick building that would serve as my residence until the morning. I asked the nurse if there was somewhere I could grab some food. I wasn't really hungry; I was actually unsure that I could stomach anything at that point, but I knew I should have something in my system. After rattling off what I could and couldn't have because of the procedure, I decided on a quick salad with a side of rice.

After wolfing down the food (I was hungrier than I thought once the food was in front of me) the nurse guided me to the front desk and filled the receptionist in. She then wished me a good night and assured me that I was in good hands. I filled out even more paperwork and was then escorted up to my room. I changed into the hospital standard - the flattering onesie. Once that was all set, a new nurse came in. One constant throughout my entire hospital experience that I noticed was that all of the staff were pleasant and warm. While I wasn't happy about my situation, the nurses and doctors sure made it as pleasant of a stay as humanly possible!

The nurse hooked me up to several monitors with half a dozen leads. I was wired by my thumb, arm and chest. She explained that I could have free reign in the room for the most part; television, bathroom, and a button if I had a question or needed assistance with anything. I had the room to myself, which was good and bad. I didn't have to worry about privacy, but at the same time, I was alone with my thoughts in an unfamiliar room. To my surprise, that evening passed very quickly and with no incident.

The morning brought the momentary confusion when I woke up in an unfamiliar area. I struggled for several seconds to figure out where I was. When I moved my right arm, I felt an uncomfortable tug. I looked down to see wires sticking out of my arm. Then I remembered the events from yesterday and it all came flooding back to me. The anxiety about what today brought also came charging right along with the memories of yesterday. I pushed the assistance button and a nurse walked in within seconds. As I had come to expect, she had a warm smile. "Good morning, Jeremy! How are you feeling today? You look better!"

"Thank you, I'm definitely feeling a bit better. I'm just wondering what the plan is for today."

"Well we're going to get you some breakfast, get you prepared for the ride to Boston and send you on your way! You have about an hour before you'll be leaving, so you have plenty of time to shower and have breakfast." The nurse started pushing buttons on the machines at my bedside. She also removed the wires from me one by one. "Alright, good to go. When you're ready, hop in the shower and let me know when you're ready for breakfast! The change of clothes your parents brought you are in the bathroom." I wasted no time in rushing into the bathroom and taking a relaxing shower.

Once I was washed and had breakfast, I was wheeled down to the ambulance. I tried objecting to the wheelchair; yeah, I needed surgery, but surely I could walk down to the truck on my own. I quickly learned that the nurse was just as firm as she was nice. After an elevator ride down to the first floor and a short distance out the main doors, I was being loaded into the truck. This was when it really started to hit me. The previous night I was able to keep myself distracted with television. But now, being helped onto a stretcher and surrounded by several medical professionals, I wasn't able to ignore the situation anymore. I had a serious condition that required a serious operation, and I needed to take it seriously and face it head-on.

The ambulance ride was a lot more pleasant than I would have imagined. The EMTs that were riding down with me gave me antibiotics that I was told were to shrink my inflamed valve and to prepare me for the surgery. It was an uneventful two-hour ride to Boston Medical Center. The EMTs were really good at keeping me light-hearted (no pun intended) with conversation throughout the ride. After being transferred to another wheelchair and handed off to another medical professional at Boston Medical Center, I thanked the EMTs for the ride and waved goodbye. A thought struck me at that point as I was being wheeled into the center. All of these doctors, nurses, EMTs and other staff deal with an enormously fast-paced work environment, help countless people through so many different maladies and setbacks, and then go home and rest to do it all over again the very next day. And the day after that. On top of all this, they all manage to make even endocarditis as smooth of a ride as is possible. Next time you see a medical professional, thank them for what they do, because they truly are miracle workers.

I went through the now-familiar process of checking in, being guided up to a room and set up in the hospital bed. I was given even more medicine and told that I would be under observation for two days before surgery on the third. Those two days, I learned, were to allow the valve to shrink as much as possible in order to ensure as simple of a surgery as possible. My parents visited on the second day, lightening my spirits and temporarily alleviating my boredom. Those two days were full of 'how are you feeling, bathroom break, drink this, bathroom break, toss back these pills, bathroom break, here's some food, how are you feeling now, bathroom break' and virtually nothing else. I know that this was necessary for the operation, but time sure passed slowly in those 48 hours.

Surgery day arrived faster than I expected. I remember being so anxious that morning. I was woken up at four in the morning. After having my vitals checked and getting a healthy dose of sedatives, I was left to lie on the stretcher and wait. The minutes dragged by, each seeming longer than the last. I was getting restless. I found myself fidgeting with my johnny gown while waiting to be brought to the operating room. After the day and a half that it seemed to take for the clock to show 5:30 A.M, I was whisked away. As I got closer to the operating room the walls got more and more bare, and the staff seemed to have a more business-like air about them. There were also more personnel in the halls. I was wheeled in front of two large doors. The nurse pushed a button on the wall and the doors creaked open, emitting a grinding squeak.

The first thing I noticed about the operating room was that it was very dark. There were no windows in the room. In fact, there was nothing on the walls at all, just a few cabinets and an odd station in the back of the room. The overhead lights were very faint. A large light hung directly over the operating table, looming like a guardian. Without any hesitation, the nurse wheeled me over to the table and helped to move me onto the cold surface. She assured me that this would all be over before I knew it and that the surgery team would be in momentarily. With a last smile, she turned and left the room.

She hadn't been gone a handful of seconds before the doors re-opened and the surgical team entered. All of the staff except for one doctor went to that odd station. That one doctor came over and briefed me on the specifics of the procedure. It would take between five and eight hours. I would be given a strong sedative that would put me out for the entire time, and I would not feel a thing. "Do you have any questions for any of us?" the doctor asked. I was feeling quite relaxed, so I simply shook my head 'no'. He said that the surgery would start within the next few minutes.

I turned my head and stared up at the ceiling, trying to count all of the small divots in the cement ceiling. The doctor picked up a needle and explained that this was the sedative I'd be getting for the surgery. He bent over the table, creating an eerie silhouette from the overhead light. I felt the slight prick of the needle. I started to get very anxious knowing that the surgery was only moments away. It was happening, no turning back now. No more time to ponder it. Thankfully, the sedatives made those thoughts and worries disappear just as quickly as they had come. The swimming image of the doctor and his team said to count from one to ten. No, it was just the one doctor that said that. "One two…" and I was out.

The next thing I remember was coming out of the fog of anesthesia. I could tell that I was conscious, but I didn't open my eyes. I was sore all over, like I had just been passed around my martial arts school as a punching bag. I also felt sick. I tried to clear my throat, but discovered there was something holding my mouth open. I pried my eyes open to investigate what it was and was met with a sight of a tube coming out of my mouth and connecting to a bedside machine. I moaned - a mixture of exasperation, pain and more exasperation. While the surgery was clearly finished, I was secretly hoping I'd be strong enough to leave the minute I came to. 'I'm a strong twenty year old, I should be able to handle this', I told myself. I tried to prop myself up, but my arms gave out and I collapsed back onto the bed. I breathed heavily, only to be reminded that it was hard to breathe with a tube down my throat.

I tilted my head to the side, searching the walls for a clock. Finding it, I squinted and saw the time: four. I had gone into surgery at six. I looked out the window of the room to see the Boston skyline, the tips of some skyscrapers poking into view. I heard a door open on the other side of the room. I strained to turn my head. I was greeted with the sight of my parents! A nurse was accompanying them. Mom rushed to my side, with Dad not far behind. Mom put her hand on my shoulder and kissed my forehead while Dad lightly ruffled my hair. It was very comforting to have them there in that moment. "How are you feeling?" Mom asked. A smile spread across her face as a tear slid down her cheek.

I tried to answer, but the tube prevented any tangible words from coming out. It sounded like I was talking into a cone with cotton in my mouth. The nurse said that I shouldn't try to talk with the tube, as it could irritate my throat. Instead, she gave me a notepad and pencil. Then she gave the three of us a rundown on the procedure.

"So you made it, Jeremy! The surgery started at six this morning and ended at two in the afternoon. We successfully replaced your inflamed valve with a new tissue valve. As you've already been told, you will need another surgery down the road due to eventual deterioration. But for now, you're good!" she exclaimed with a big smile, holding her hand up for a high five. Thankfully, she held it close to me so it didn't take too much effort. "So how are you feeling right now? Anything uncomfortable or hurting?"

"Throat is sore, tube uncomfortable. Feel slightly ill," I wrote on the notepad and showed it to her. The nurse stated that the ill feeling is a common reaction to the anesthesia, as was the sore throat. She also said that the tube would be taken out in several hours after I was cleared from the ICU, and that it was just a precaution to make sure there were no complications or issues from the surgery. She continued to explain that once I was cleared from the ICU, I would remain at the hospital for several days of post-operation observation. As much as I just wanted to get back to my regular routine, I knew that a heart valve surgery was nothing to rush through.

Even though I had been put under for almost twelve hours, I was exhausted. The nurse finished explaining all that my parents and I needed to know and then left the room. It was good to have my parents at my side.

The condition and surgery had been such a quick series of events that it was nice to know that for the immediate future, it was over. I would need a few days to recover, but the worst was over. The only direction I could go from here was up.

I had as much of a conversation as I could with my parents using the notepad. They both filled the time with small talk and funny stories from the past few days. After about an hour, they got up to leave, saying that they'd be back down to pick me up once I was cleared from recovery.

The very first morning after the operation, I was already feeling better than I had prior to the surgery. The next few days were full of small, minute tests, along with getting a grip on my body again. Some tasks involved simply holding my arm out and the nurses running tests, always scribbling away on their clipboards. Others involved walking around the ward. In between these tests, I poured over several books that my parents had brought for me. On the morning of the third day post-surgery, I was cleared to go home! I called my parents and filled them in on the good news, saying that they could come down and get me whenever they were free. My mother was overjoyed at my speedy recovery, saying that she was on her way immediately. I heard the sound of a car engine starting in the background as she hung up, suggesting that dad had bolted to the car at hearing the news.

I made my way back into my room and relaxed on the bed, interlacing my fingers behind my head as a smile lit up across my face. I must have dozed off, because the next thing I knew I was being shaken awake by my mom. "Alright champ, let's go," she said with a light punch to my arm. I got up from the bed and followed her out of the room, giving my temporary living quarters one last look-over before closing the door behind me.

When checking out, I was given a prescription for antibiotics that I would be taking for the next six weeks. Also, I was to be on home rest for those six weeks. The home rest was a tough pill to swallow, but it had to be done. I already informed my boss of the situation and he was very understanding and flexible, for which I was very thankful. I had also informed Mr. Hardy, who told me to take as much time as I needed and that I would be missed in the dojo in the meantime.

I held the door open for my mother as we left the hospital. Dad had snagged a great parking spot right near the main entrance, so the walk to the car was short. I looked up at the sky as we made our way to the car. The sun was shining brightly that day, with a clear blue sky. There were clouds way off in the distance, but those would take time to make their way in. Right now, the skies were clear as could be.

Just like my path in life at that time. In ten years or so I would require additional heart surgery to maintain the valve. But for now, the road was clear and bright for me. I had a healthy heart, a job, a passion for martial arts, and my whole life ahead of me. I was ready to take on the world. With these thoughts and outlooks brightening up my spirit, I opened the car door, sat down and buckled up for the ride home.

Part Two – Heart Throbs, Young at Heart and Heart Failure

Chapter Five
What the Heart Wants

The following six weeks of home rest were bittersweet. While I felt better with each passing day, I was confined to the house. To avoid just lounging around, I would often work my forms and techniques from martial arts in the air. It wasn't the same as being in the dojo with a partner, but it was the next best thing. Between burying myself in books, practicing martial arts and having friends over, the six weeks of recovery went by faster than expected. Almost two months after that terrible day that had been capped off with the news that I had a potentially fatal heart disorder, I was fully recovered from having open-heart surgery. My body had reacted exceptionally well to the tissue valve with no complications, and a speedy recovery. A simple check-up at the doctors and I was cleared to resume my everyday life unrestrained.

I was anxious to jump right back into the swing of things. The day after being cleared, I was back at work in retail and working out (conservatively) at Bodyworks. I was careful not to push myself too hard or too quickly and undo all of the time I had spent recovering. After two additional weeks of gradually easing myself into my full routine of work, martial arts and friends, I was feeling fully recovered. Healed. One hundred percent.

Over the next several years, I kept myself busy with work and martial arts. If I wasn't at my regular job or working for my father's construction business, I was at the dojo or hanging out with friends. Eat, sleep, work, martial arts, work, friends, work, martial arts and work was my life in my early twenties. I climbed my way up the promotional ladder to become the assistant manager of the Abercrombie and Fitch store that I had worked in for years. This was an exciting new avenue for me. While I was still working at the same location doing the same day-to -day exercises that a retail job requires, I started learning the ins and outs of being a manager. I learned what worked and what didn't through old-fashioned trial and error: the best way to customize orientation for a new employee based on their personality, the most efficient communication methods with the store employees I supervised, and the basics of business bookkeeping…all skills that I gained during my time as a manager. These are skills that can only be learned effectively, in my opinion, on the job and through experience. While I was told how to do all of these things, the only way I actually grasped them was to jump into the trenches of management and learn how to best apply them.

After Abercrombie and Fitch, I started working at J Crew, another retail store. I quickly rose to the position of manager of the store. I noticed that my experience as manager of that store was easier than at Abercrombie not because the stores were different from one another, but because I had figured out what worked and what didn't as a manager. To this day, I still use the lessons I learned from managing these two stores.

While working in retail was enjoyable, working construction and labor for my father was even more so. Working in retail showed me the ropes of being a successful and effective manager, and working with my Dad taught me hard working values and what it meant to put in a hard day's physical work. Regardless of the season or weather, there was always something to be done. The spring and summer brought the need for sweeping parking lots, cleaning yards and building peoples' spring projects for them. Fall was raking and more raking, along with leaf blowing here and there. Winter required lots of shoveling and clearing driveways, roof raking and other general snow removal. Whatever we were doing, I was beat at the end of the day. Some days, I was so tired after work that I wouldn't even go to the dojo, an activity that I normally did on a daily basis.

Working with my father was very rewarding. Not only did it bring us even closer together, but it made me appreciate him that much more. He is one of the hardest working men I've ever met, and what he did for his business and our family was and still is simply amazing. Day in and day out, he ran his business and was right on the front lines doing the jobs himself. He has always been selfless, never seeking out recognition or looking for praise. I have always strived to be just as honorable of a man as he is.

Seeing how much my father loved his business and loved the field of work he was in got me thinking about my own future. Sure, I was making a decent amount between managing J Crew and working in the construction business. But my dreams of working with fitness training in some facet were as fresh as ever. I would daydream every now and then while at work about what I could become. A personal trainer? Gym owner? Sponsored athlete? These were all attractive options. I wanted to find that something that made me tick, that made me as happy and satisfied as my father was with his business.

Though I dreamed of the possibilities related to a fitness career, I had additional career options on my plate. I had a real estate license along with my personal trainer certification. These were the means to pursue two entirely different career paths. I knew I couldn't do both, so I had to choose. After pondering both options for months, doing research on both fields and talking the options over with my parents, I decided that I was going to follow my passion and build a career in the fitness industry. This was easier said than done. I had to find a place that I could work as a member of a staff at gym, or lease space at a gym and work with my own clientele. This turned out to be quite a challenge. While I looked around at local gyms for an open position I continued the construction work with my father.

One day during August of 2003, I was taking advantage of a day off from work to hang out with my best friend and his girlfriend. We were at their apartment in Manchester, exchanging small talk over food and a football game. Talk moved to my recently ended relationship. It wasn't a bad breakup, but I also didn't want to talk about it all that much. Suddenly, my best friend sat up straight and exclaimed, "Hey, wait a minute! Jeremy, there's this awesome girl that lives across the street from us. We're going to introduce you to her!"

"Whoa, slow down there. I just got out of a relationship a week ago," I pointed out.

"Yeah, well Brook also just got out of a relationship. Looks like it's meant to be," my friend joked. Having no objection to it, I agreed to meet Brook. The next day we had been set up for a blind date. We would be having dinner at a local bar that night. I rushed through work with Dad and finished the job a half hour ahead of schedule, which gave me ample time to head home and tidy up. At 5:30, I was heading out the door to the bar.

I made sure to get there earlier than normal. I would have felt pretty sheepish if I got there and Brook had already been sitting at a table. Once there, I stood outside and waited for her. Sure enough, she pulled into the parking lot only two minutes after I had arrived; my friend had described her car to me so I would know what to look for. 'Whew, good thing I got here ahead of time!' I thought. When she got out of her car and started walking toward me, I immediately noticed the presence she had about her. Just through how she carried herself, I could tell she was a strong-willed, confident woman. I waved to her, which prompted a smile. Oh man, her smile lit up the entire parking lot. Her light brown hair fell neatly over her shoulders and waved in the breeze as she walked. I noticed my heart beat a bit faster. She was certainly as good looking as my friend had said. We introduced ourselves, exchanged pleasantries and headed into the bar for dinner.

We hit it off from the start. Our personalities clicked perfectly and we were both smiling and laughing constantly throughout the entire date. After that, we knew that we had a special connection and that we had the potential for an amazing relationship. And sure enough, we only got closer from there. Our first month together we were inseparable. We both enjoyed each other's company so much that three months into our relationship, we made the decision to move in together. This was a drastic move for me, as I'd never lived anywhere besides with my parents, in the house I grew up in. But I felt good about it. We were committed to each other and this next step felt natural.

Brook Woodward, Jeremy's wife

"The first date that I had with Jeremy was very special. Even from just that first date, I could tell that he was quite different from anyone else I had dated in the past. Just from the first several dates, I knew that we would be together; it felt like we were made for one another. The best part was from the beginning, I felt secure in the relationship unlike anything in the past. I think that's what set Jeremy apart."

A year later, Brook and I were as happy as on our first date. We were with each other for who we were as individuals, not for each other's jobs or money. In reality, Brook made (and still makes) the big bucks between us! Having been together for over a year, we decided it was time to reach another milestone. We got engaged in the fall of 2004 and were married in the fall of 2005. Everything was falling into place. I was pursuing a career in what I loved with the love of my life by my side.

Chapter Six
A New Experience

As the summer of 2006 rolled around, I had made no further progress in landing a job as a personal trainer or fitness coach. This didn't stop me from being as physically active as possible. In addition to continuing construction work, I went out for morning runs here and there, and rode my bike whenever I could. I had built up a formidable amount of endurance, and would sometimes go for thirty mile bike rides.

On a nice summer day after a bike ride with several friends and my wife, we went back to a friend's house for a cookout and bonfire, an awesome way to end the day. We were all laughing and joking around the fire with great food and great company. We were talking about everything: work, random stories and everything in between. At one point, one of our friends told a story about his cousin Joe who had just completed his first triathlon. At the end of his story, he turned to me and said, "You know, you should do a triathlon, Jeremy. There's one around here coming up that Joe is going to be doing, you could do it. You already have the bike riding and running down."

I scoffed at his idea. "No way, man. Between work and everything I don't have time for something like that."

"Sure you do! You just spent all of today on a bike ride that was longer than the distance for an average bike ride in a triathlon. Then it's just running and swimming."

"*Just* running and swimming? Yeah, not a chance."

"Come on man, I dare you to try it. I'm not saying to become a pro, just try it! The worst that happens is that you get your ass handed to you." This comment was met with laughs from the whole group, including Brook. One of my big character flaws is that I'm like a little kid with dares. If someone genuinely challenges me to do something physical (within reason, of course), I have a hard time saying no.

"You know what? Fine, I'll do it. I'll start training for it. When is it, a few months? I think I could cram enough training in that time." My friend smirked and leaned forward in his seat.

"It's in ten days."

Everyone around the fire looked at me, waiting for my response. I took a bite of my food and nodded my head. Through my mouthful, I mumbled, "No worries, I got this." My friends and wife didn't look surprised at all. They knew to expect this brass type of decision making from me. "You're right bud, I already have two-thirds of the triathlon down, I just need to prepare for swimming."

"Awesome, I expect you to smoke the rest of the field," my friend said sarcastically. We laughed it off and continued with our night without mentioning the triathlon again.

Swimming dominated my free time over the next ten days. I practiced different strokes, figuring out what would work best for the long distance swim and what to do for a quick rest. I knew the swim would be the hardest part of the race by far. I was already conditioned for and used to both the running and biking. Not only was I unfamiliar with the swimming portion but it was also the first part of the race. I made sure to practice for this by either running or biking immediately after each training swim, sometimes doing both. While I knew competing in this triathlon on such short notice would be a challenge, I was confident that I could finish the race.

Brook and I decided to make a weekend trip out of the race. It was in Massachusetts on a Sunday, so she and I headed down on Friday morning. It was only an hour drive from our hotel so Friday and Saturday consisted of sightseeing, training, and more sightseeing. As the start drew closer and closer, I was feeling more and more anxious. I wasn't nervous, but I was eager to race. Previously, I had only competed in martial arts competitions and basketball games. This was a whole new frontier. And I knew nothing about it.

To better understand what I was in for, I called a friend of mine who was a sort of guru on anything and everything sports related. I told him that I was entering my first triathlon in less than 24 hours and asked if he had any advice or pointers for me. He answered my question with a question, asking what I had done for training. I recited my training up to that point, adding in that I had taken on this challenge on less than two weeks notice. As I expected, this last statement drew a surprised reaction from my friend. He laughed and asked if I was kidding. When he realized I was serious, he gave me some advice that I still hold dear to this day.

"So you've done martial arts competitions and basketball tournaments, Jeremy. With these two disciplines, you practice certain moves and drills over and over, then simply go out and execute them just as you've practiced. Maybe you have to change the game plan in the middle of the event, but for the most part nothing changes, except the spectators. This is not at all true with triathlons. Even with the impressive training you've managed to do in a week, an actual triathlon is entirely different than the training to prepare for it. While the biking, running and swimming are essentially carbon copies of your training, the environment is the real challenge. You're surrounded by a mob of other people doing the same thing as you. Hundreds of people swimming in the ocean at the same time, all going in the same direction, is more mentally challenging than physically. The biking aspect is similar. You're surrounded by people passing you and you're passing others. Forget about the mess if there's an accident. As for the run, you're already beat and have to run for what will probably seem like forever at your first triathlon. The name of the game is to keep a cool head. Get tunnel vision. Zone everything else out. Someone's thrashing in the water three feet from you as they pass you? Don't pay attention to them. Someone is gasping as you pass them on the bike? Keep on pushing."

I thanked my friend for the insight into what I was in for the next day. Some last-minute training on Saturday was followed by a nice dinner with my wife at an upscale restaurant. With a stomach full of excellent food and butterflies, I headed to bed and dreamed about the challenges that Sunday would bring.

Just as the forecasts had predicted, Sunday was a gorgeous New England summer day, pleasantly warm with partly cloudy skies. I ate breakfast overlooking the Massachusetts coastline. Several boats were skimming across the Atlantic, bobbing up and down as the waves morphed around their edges. Closer to shore, families were playing in the shallows. Some were sliding across the water on skim boards or boogie boards, others tossed beach balls and frisbees back and forth, and still others jumped around in the water with waves crashing around them. In just a few hours, I'd be splashing through the same water several miles away.

The drive to the beginning of the triathlon was nerve-wracking. Even though I was excited for the race, I still had no clue how it would play out. Despite all of the advice I received from my friend and all of the training I had done, I still felt like I had no idea what I was in store for. Before I knew it, the beach came into view out of nowhere. One minute the road was shadowed by tree cover and winding back and forth, the next minute the trees parted and sunlight poured through the windshield.

I was amazed at how many people were there. There was still over half an hour before the start of the race and there were hundreds of competitors spread out across the beach. Spectators lined the road, snapping pictures and shouting to some of the racers.

This race was a sprint distance triathlon. Scheduled to start with a half-mile swim, the race transitions to a fifteen mile bike ride and ends with a 3.6 mile run. 'Piece of cake, I've done a half-mile swim this week. I got this,' I told myself, trying to boost my confidence.

We parked and walked over to the registration table. I had pre-registered, so I only had to give my name and not worry about the hassle of filling out any forms. I was given my race tag and a 'good luck!' from the woman who was running the table. I grabbed a last swig of water, a kiss from Brook, and stepped onto the beach to stretch out. I ran through a mental checklist as my feet sunk into the sand. My bike and shoes were all set at the end of the swim. I had my goggles. I was ready to go.

As I walked among my fellow competitors, I noticed that every one of them had a sharp-looking wetsuit on. I, on the other hand, was wearing basketball shorts that were two sizes too big for me, and no shirt. I was mentally kicking myself for not thinking to ask about what to wear. While I had baggy shorts, these guys had tight, full-body wetsuits. My cheap dollar store goggles were also mismatched against their tinted, expensive-looking goggles. 'This is CRAZY,' I thought. I figured I could just show up after a few weeks of practice and keep up with everyone else because of the shape I was in. I was starting to see more and more that this was not the case.

I saw some of the competitors walking down into the water and splashing themselves, then walking right back out. I thought that they were acclimating their bodies to the water so it wouldn't be as much of a shock to the system when the race started. Deciding to take a page out of their books, I strolled down the beach into the water and started splashing water over my legs and arms, trying not to let the stares get to me.

"First triathlon?"

I turned around to see who the voice belonged to. An older gentleman was walking down to me. He was probably in his late fifties based on his predominantly white hair. He was tall, at least six feet. His toned muscles rippled through his skinny frame, seeming ready to burst through his wetsuit. When I pictured what I thought a fit triathlete would look like, it was this man in front of me. He extended his hand and said, "The name's Henry."

"Jeremy," I replied as I shook his hand. His grip was like iron. "Uh, yeah, it's pretty obvious huh?" He chuckled and took a step back.

"You look more like a skater than anything right now. And the lack of a wetsuit also gives you away," Henry joked.

"Well will I be okay? I mean, what difference will not having a wetsuit make?"

"Yeah, you'll be fine. You'll be colder and your swimming won't be as efficient, but you should be fine. Just a tip: don't get distracted by the others when you're swimming. Don't feel that you need to yield for someone or make way for them, they will move around you." He asked about my experience with swimming, biking and running. I shared my training outline with him. When I told him the background about the dare and my crammed training sessions, he raised his eyebrows in surprise.

"Think of it like this. The biking and running are pretty straightforward. Use the ride as your break, get a solid pace and hold it. It's better to have more in the tank than you think you need for the run. Remember that, and you'll do great. Enjoy it. Don't take yourself too seriously, especially your first time!"

"Well thanks a lot Henry. I really appreciate it. It's nice to see a friendly face here, I feel like a black sheep with all the stares I'm getting."

"Oh don't let that get to you. Most people show up with some type of a race suit, but I have to say, I don't know many people that would tackle an obstacle like this for the first time on two weeks' notice. Good luck today, Jeremy.

Have fun!" With a parting handshake, Henry turned around and jogged back up the beach.

As I splashed more water over my legs, I looked around at the other competitors. Lots of them were in the water so that it was just above their waists. While watching the crowds, I noticed something odd: none of the racers were talking to one another, and they were just standing still. They didn't even acknowledge one another. Randomly, they would then walk out of the water and back onto the beach. After puzzling over this anomaly for several seconds, I understood what was going on. They were peeing in the water; masses of racers had made their way out into the lake just to relieve themselves. Disgusted, I stood up and half-ran, half-jogged out of the water. I heard a voice come over the speakers announcing the two minute warning for the race and made my way over to the starting area.

I put my goggles on, adjusting the straps to make them as comfortable as possible. I looked at the people I was surrounded with. One person was bent over and swinging his arms back and forth. Lots of people were doing something to keep moving, either shifting feet or hopping in place. A sharp breeze came in from the ocean just as the loudspeaker came back on. After welcoming the competitors and the crowd to the race, the rules and order of events were laid out. Again I thought to myself, 'This is CRAZY. What was I thinking, getting myself into this?' Before I knew it, the announcer told us to take to the starting line.

I lined up next to my fellow racers. My heart was pounding with anticipation. I took several deep breaths to calm myself down. The announcer started to count down. I knew what I was about to do was insane, that I'd be pushed to my limit. The starting sound erupted through my thoughts, startling me. Racers ran ahead of me and plunged into the water. I leapt into action and followed, jumping into the ocean to begin my first triathlon.

Despite testing the water beforehand, it was a shock to my system. I came up gasping and struggling to get a bearing. The already choppy water had turned into a frenzy of movement and sound. The clap of people moving through the water matched the splashes from their arms chopping through the waves. I felt rushed, like I had to move faster in order to catch up to the racers in front of me. I quickly became winded, which in hindsight was probably more mental than anything. The breeze cut at my skin as I swam in the general direction of the checkpoint. The advice I had gotten was spot on; the environment and setting got to me - quickly.

I was completely gassed after only about 150 yards of swimming. I was only a fraction of the way through the swim and I wanted to quit. It wasn't because my heart wasn't in it. I felt like I was going to drown. Having to keep such a sharp eye on my surroundings so as to not swim into someone, while also swimming at a constantly fast pace, was so much harder than I imagined. But I knew I couldn't quit, I just had to keep pushing through and persevere. Right as I got my head back in the race, my shorts slipped off! I scrambled to reach underwater and pull them back up as I treaded water. While looking down to try and tie the waist tighter, my goggles filled up with water. Frustrated, I quickly lifted them and allowed the water to run out, making sure I made a tight seal afterward. Once my shorts and goggles seemed to be all set, I let out a growl of effort and continued on with the swim.

Halfway through the swim, I was devoid of energy. I switched to a backstroke because I was afraid that if I stopped to tread water I wouldn't be able to continue. My shorts had slipped off two more times. The dollar store goggles weren't faring much better, the water that was constantly gathering in the bottom was getting more and more irritating. When I was swimming in rivers and lakes for practice, the water didn't bother me if it got inside the goggles. However, the salt water was a different story. It stung at my eyes and irritated them. Most of the racers were ahead of me. A select few looked to be already climbing out of the water and transitioning, whereas I still had about a third of the swim left.

Brook Woodward

"Even though Jeremy had basically no time to prepare for the triathlon, I had faith in him. With the swim portion, I couldn't differentiate between any of the racers; all were wearing white swim caps. I saw one of the racers bobbing in the back of the group and flailing around like they didn't know where they were. I remember thinking, 'oh man, please don't be Jeremy.' Sure enough, when that person stopped to tread water and gasp for breath, I saw that it was my husband."

Roughly an eternity later, I was nearing the checkpoint for the swim. The shore was getting closer. I gained a second wind once I could make out details on the shore. The sandy mini-beach with several large rocks scattered on either side of it was shadowed by overhanging pine trees, looming over competitors as they jogged out of the water. I was one of the last to finish the swim out of several hundred racers. There was a group of spectators standing behind a barrier, cheering on the winded racers as they emerged from the water. A stand with water was on the side of the beach, just before a stand with bikes. I scanned for my bike as I swam in. Not seeing it, I gave up and tried to find my footing. My legs almost gave out when I tried to stand up. Steadying myself, I made my way out of the water and started taking huge gulps of air. I had done it. A fraction of a way through the swim I thought for sure that I was going to drown. But somehow I had finished the swim. I was so proud of myself! But now it was time to buckle down and finish the race.

I grabbed a cup of water on my way to the bike rack and flushed the salty taste out of my mouth. I quickly realized that I had no idea how to transition as smooth as the other racers. Everyone was stripping off their wetsuits, something that I didn't need to do. I jogged over to the rack and found my bike, haphazardly throwing my shoes on. As I jumped on my bike, I turned back to the water I had dragged myself out of just a few moments before. There were only a handful of racers behind me, the farthest back still about three minutes away from shore. I wanted to make up some ground throughout the rest of the race. I knew going into the race that I wasn't going to be right up at the top with the elite racers, but I certainly hadn't expected to be at the bottom. I pushed off and started pedaling, intent on catching up to the rest of the racers now that I was in my element.

For the biking portion of the triathlon, we had to ride a loop that had been mapped out. The loop was only six miles, so we had to complete two and a half loops for the fifteen total miles. There was a turnoff back at the start of the loop that led to the checkpoint that we would take once we had finished two laps. After that, we would drop the bikes and transition into the last segment of the race.

The start of the ride was cold, with the wind rushing across my wet skin. Once I was dry I started to warm up from the sun cutting through the trees here and there. It didn't take long for me to find my rhythm. I set an aggressive pace, intent on making up time from the swim. I started passing people that had passed me during the swim. Again, I saw that Henry was right. The ride felt like a breeze compared to the swim even though it wasn't any less physically demanding.

The first loop went by quickly. Volunteers were holding out

paper cups full of water at the water stand. The racers would grab a cup without stopping and either drain it or pour it over their heads. They would then toss the empty cups off to the side of the road, where more volunteers quickly cleaned up the mess. I grabbed two cups of water on my way past the starting point of the loop. I poured the first one over my head, quickly tossed the cup and grabbed another, drinking it in three large gulps. After the brief distraction of the crowds at the loop and the cheering spectators, it was back to the loop for my second lap.

Since I now knew the twists and turns, I was able to zone out a little bit and analyze where I was during my second loop. I was feeling really spent, but I was at the point where I could just keep on whatever pace I set until I was done. The transition from riding to running concerned me, as I'd get out of my zone that I was in and have to focus on a quick transition. This would take me off of my pace, and fatigue might begin to set in. I tried to focus in on the rest of the ride and not let my mind wander to the variables that I'd face in a few minutes, but I felt my attention drifting back to the transition and how I was going to keep pace through the run to the finish line.

I passed through the water stand and spectators again before I knew it. I grabbed a water cup and tossed it back and kept right on riding, not losing any focus. I was almost done with the loops, and then I could transition.

'WAIT!' I half thought, half screamed. I had such tunnel vision during the loop that I had missed the turnoff for the transition! I threw out several choice swear words as I careened to a stop, turned my bike around and sped back to the turnoff. I felt so sheepish as I pedaled back, seeing as I was the only one heading backwards on the loop. I got yelled at by several competitors, and told that I was going the wrong way. Even though I noticed all of these, I didn't pay them any mind. I was flying back to the checkpoint of the loop as fast as I could. Thankfully I hadn't gone too far past the turnoff – I saw it after only a minute. I took it without braking and almost wiped out. I rode for another two minutes up the turnoff route to the transition point for the last leg of the race.

As I approached the end of the riding portion of the race, I thought about all of the time that I had lost. I had made up a considerable amount of time during the ride, but then threw a chunk of it away by not paying attention to the course as much as I should have. I wasn't doing nearly as well as I thought I would be. The swim was a disaster, I spaced out on the ride, and now I was fumbling with getting off of my bike and transitioning to the run. My foot got caught on my bike and I came close to falling on my face on the pavement. Through clumsy hops and lots of arm waving, I somehow ended up on two feet and took off past the checkpoint, grabbing a cup of water as I started the three and a half mile run.

I started my run with the optimistic thought that I couldn't mess up on the run like I had with the swim and ride. Even though I hadn't performed as I had hoped I would and had messed up to this point, I was having a blast. I smiled and focused back in on finishing the race on a good note.

The running was going great, and I got into a decent groove about a mile and a half into the run. I knew I was coming up on the halfway point.. I rounded a curve in the road and saw a barrier set up with a race official sitting against it. He turned to face me as I ran up to him. "Hey, what's this?" I asked, confused as to why the road was blocked. I definitely hadn't run over three miles, so this wasn't the finish. There were no spectators either, so I was baffled. I jogged to a stop and leaned on the barrier.

"You're in the triathlon?"

"Yeah," I stated. The race official started laughing until he coughed.

"You're not messing with me?! Buddy, you went the wrong way at the transition. You went to the left. You were supposed to run right. Nobody called out to you that you were going the wrong way? No one was running ahead of you for you to follow?"

I kept shaking my head, too out of breath and ticked off to answer. "I'm sorry man. Unfortunately, this means that you're disqualified from the race. My buddy can give you a lift to the finish line if you want so you don't have to walk." As much as I hated the thought, I grudgingly accepted the offer. I didn't know what to feel; one moment I wanted to get up in the race official's face and yell at him for not making the turn obvious back at the checkpoint, the next I wanted to scream in frustration. I forced myself to shovel these angry emotions down as I hopped the barrier and took a seat in an ATV that was parked off to the side of the road. Anger gave way to disappointment, and I felt defeated. I had put in lots of effort and practice into this race, only to mess it all up and not even get to finish. The race official I was riding with seemed to be able to sense my disappointment and offered me some encouraging words.

"Was this your first triathlon?" I nodded my head in acknowledgement. "Well look at it this way. Before today, you had never done a half-mile swim with hundreds of competitors. You had never done a fifteen mile bike ride through an unfamiliar area while racing against others. And you were hauling as you ran up on us at the barrier, so you had an awesome pace going. Even though today didn't turn out like you wanted, hopefully it was good enough for you to get back in the saddle and give it another try soon."

I let his words sink in. I was still simmering about my performance. The more I thought about it, the more his words made sense. What I had just done was so incredibly hard, but I had fun doing it. The people involved in the triathlon, both competitors and volunteers, were absolutely amazing. What some of the racers were able to do physically was unbelievable. The enthusiasm shown from everyone was contagious.

When I got to the finish line, I found Brook in the crowd. She looked concerned, asking if I had injured myself somehow. When I told her the chain of events that had led to my unusual arrival at the finish line, she laughed. She tried to hide it by covering her mouth, but I could see the look in her eyes that said, "Really? Really, Jeremy?" I had to laugh along with her. Now that a little time had passed since my unique ending to the race and my heart rate was back to normal, the whole situation was comical. We stayed in the crowd for a few minutes to watch several of my fellow racers cross the finish line. After that, we made our way to where the workers had moved the bikes, loaded mine on top of the car and began the commute back to New Hampshire.

Brook Woodward

"I couldn't believe that Jeremy didn't finish the race, because the bike ride and run were much more his element than the swim. When I saw that he had finished the swim, I was sure he had the rest of the race. Even though he was a little bummed out that he didn't finish, he loved it and was excited to train and do more events like this one."

On the ride back, my wife and I talked almost exclusively about the triathlon. She was very curious. I gave her a play-by-play of everything I had done, including the details of my baggy shorts and goggles during the swim. She laughed through the entire story. I told her about how cool the entire experience was and how I wanted to get better and do another race soon. "Next year, I'm going to do more races like this. I'm going to train from now until then so I will be much more prepared than I was today," I told her.

This style of race was a new challenge for me. I had n been as physically or mentally challenged as I was in that triathlon. The swim was a major obstacle to get over. The bike ride required much more focus than I anticipated, and I had even managed to screw up something as simple as a run. The week and a half that I had to prepare and train for that race had moved me out of my comfort zone. I was intrigued. This new challenge was daring me to conquer it. Triathlons had always seemed crazy to me. And sure enough, they were even crazier after having done (er, attempted) one. But that challenge was like bait for me. I wanted to better myself and prove that this was something I could do, and do well. I didn't just want to try another triathlon, I wanted to train and own a triathlon. Brook supported the idea and encouraged me. Over the next several months, I intensified my workouts, honed my training and focused like a madman. Triathlons were my new obsession. I had gotten a taste, and I wanted more. I had no idea that I was taking a bite out of something that would eventually become an integral part of my entire being.

Chapter Seven
History Repeats Itself

Following the triathlon, I intensified my training and started working toward my goal of finishing a triathlon. In the meantime, I had lots of other responsibilities on my plate. For starters, my job search finally paid off. Five years after I earned my personal fitness trainer certificate and only three months after my first attempt at a triathlon, I came across a privately owned gym in the Concord area. After several meetings and piles of paperwork, I leased space and time from the gym and started my career as a fitness trainer!

I was happier than I can describe. I was finally doing what I had been itching to do for so many years. My passion was finally my job. My father had always told me to seek out a job doing what I love, and I had achieved it. When I broke the news to Brook that I had been successful in leasing space and time from the gym, she was just as enthused as I was and encouraged me to run with it. Just as I was doing more and more for myself, I was excited to help people get physically fit and improve their lifestyles. Whether it was several pounds, a dress size or packing on the muscle, I was up for the challenge of assisting and guiding people in attaining their fitness goals.

Over the next four months, I built up a large clientele. I was doing much better than I could have hoped. I was always busy at work doing what I loved. The money was very different from when I had been working odd jobs for the construction company. I missed working with my father, but he practically pushed me off the job site when I told him that I had scored the job, telling me to get to my dream job and not look back. The support I received from Brook and my parents in this time meant so much to me. Everything in my life improved because of my new job; my training, my overall attitude, and even my bottom line.

It was four months into my new career. Winter had come to a close and spring was in the air. It was late March. In New Hampshire, this time of year brings melting snow banks, streams running high, trees budding and birds returning to backyard feeders. One day after work, I felt sick, the kind of sick feeling one gets from a nasty cold that affects the whole body. I took the usual cold medicine over the next week, but the sickness persisted. My symptoms didn't improve, but they also didn't worsen.

The next month brought more of the same from my extended cold. I always loaded up on medicine before going in to work. Who wants a trainer or coach that is always tired and hacking up a lung? I made sure to hide my illness as much as I could while at work, but it was very evident no matter what I tried. I wasn't able to perform at my normal level at work or in my training, which was very frustrating. Stress started to build from the obstacles this sickness presented at work. This stress, in turn, took an additional toll on me, and the cycle slowly but noticeably compounded over and over.

A bike ride at the end of April showed me that I should take a closer look at this cold of mine. I was riding with some friends that had joined in on my training sessions. We had all ridden this route many times and were conditioned well. We were able to hold an in-depth conversation during the ride. At one point, there was a steep hill that was always grueling to climb. As my friends had seen recently, the cold affected my performance during training, so they threw back a, 'we'll wait for you at the top!' as they pedaled ahead of me, knowing that I'd take considerably more time to make it up the hill. As the incline became steeper, my friends pulled farther ahead of me.

I was already winded. But I'd pedaled up this hill well over a hundred times, including several times since I had come down with the cold. I gritted my teeth and pushed myself into overdrive, fighting to keep as much momentum as I could. Gradually I lost speed, which made the climb even harder. I had slowed to a crawl, rocking my bike side to side to avoid losing momentum altogether. I was only halfway up the hill and fighting for every rotation of my wheels. My legs were screaming from effort, my entire body was shaking. Finally I lost all speed and I had to put my foot out to brace myself. I was exhausted and still at least a hundred feet from the top of the hill.

My friends started laughing and called down to me, throwing out sarcastic comments and light jeers. I tried to mask my embarrassment with a smile and shake of my head. Inside, I was so upset with myself. I had been up that hill many times and never had an issue. I walked my bike up the rest of the way. I convinced myself that my lack of performance was due to the stress from work combined with the monster cold I couldn't seem to shake. Once I reached the top, I endured several more jabs from my friends. They pointed out that I was the one in the group that did this kind of thing for work. We sparred with words for a minute or so and then continued on the rest of the ride.

After we finished the ride, I made my way to work. As I had grown to expect, work was stressful. I felt awful, I wasn't as in tune to my clients as I should have been, and I wasn't my normal energetic self. When I got home that night, I vented to my wife about my day, filling her in on the hill incident and the headaches of work. As she had many times before, she urged me to go and see a doctor. And as I had done many times before, I stubbornly refused, saying that I'd heal up in a couple days. Brook countered with the fact that I had been saying that constantly for the past two weeks. I dismissed the idea of a doctor's visit. It was nothing serious, just a stubborn cold, and I needed to prove that I was more stubborn than this cold.

That night as I lay in bed, I noticed my heart was racing. My chest was pumping like I was back on the hill from earlier in the day. I tried to ignore it and fall asleep, hoping that it would go away, but to no avail. I was left lying awake knowing that something was seriously wrong. But as I always managed to do, I convinced myself that whatever this was would clear up on its own.

Unfortunately, this would not prove to be the case.

Two weeks later, the cold was still with me and worse than ever. A week after the incident in bed, I experienced the same irregularly fast heart beat an hour after completing my routine morning run before work. Again, I related this to the ever-increasing stress. I decided I needed a break from the monotony. That night I suggested to Brook that we take a short vacation to Maine for a long weekend. She liked the idea and started planning out a fun weekend for us.

It was great to get away for several days. Though I missed the training and my clients at the gym, I had needed some relaxation time. The time Brook and I got to spend together was just as great. The whole time that we were up in Maine, however, I didn't feel myself. I was constantly fatigued. I felt in a haze. No matter how much I willed myself to overcome the cold, I felt dragged down. I felt beaten down. My head was always pounding. My chest hurt when I took in a deep breath. My stomach was constantly upset. Even my appetite was starting to be affected, as Brook pointed out when we went out to eat and I could barely finish an appetizer.

June brought more bad health news. At the beginning of the month, I noticed that I had put on a significant amount of weight.

This didn't correlate with my declining appetite, so I was puzzled. To add to the confusion, all of the weight was on my stomach and thighs. I showed Brook, and she replied with her usual 'go to the doctor' response. She was starting to get fed up that I was refusing to get checked out. Until now, I was steadfast about not going to the doctor. But this was concerning to me. I immediately stopped work the first week of June. I knew now that this wasn't about to just fade away. I needed to be careful, especially with my health history.

At the beginning of May, I had weighed 180 pounds, a very tone and fit weight for someone of my size and stature. Alarmingly, I weighed just shy of 200 pounds on the third week of June. At one point when I tentatively pressed my hand into my leg where I had gained weight my hand formed around what felt like built-up fluid or silly putty. The skin was a deep shade of yellow. I was now officially worried. The cold had been one thing. Twenty pounds of weight gain in three weeks was an entirely different matter. I was in trouble and I didn't know how or why.

Because of my weight gain, I chose not to drive whenever I could avoid it. One day in the middle of June, I woke up in a fog, feeling very disoriented. I had felt like this before, but couldn't remember when. I remembered Brook leaving for work in the morning as I was making breakfast. Looking back, the next thing I remember from that day was being in an elevator. I was so confused. I knew I hadn't driven, so I had no idea where I was. The elevator doors suddenly slid open and bright sunlight poured in through large glass windows from the room in front of me. I shielded my eyes with my hand. I examined my surroundings and realized the elevator had opened up to the top of a building. I was now really confused. I didn't recognize my surroundings. For a split second I wondered if I was dreaming, but quickly ruled that out. I slowly emerged from the elevator and walked into what looked like a waiting area in an office building. There was no one else in the room except for the receptionist. She looked up and smiled. “Hello, can I help you?” she asked politely.

“Uhm, where am I?” I asked bluntly.

“Sorry, do you mean this floor or this building? Wait, don’t you work in the gym in the basement?”

Now it made sense, sort of. ‘This must be the top floor of my work building,’ I concluded. The gym that I leased space from was situated in the basement of a seven story office building. I must have meant to go down in the elevator and just hit the wrong button in the elevator.

But why was I at work? I’ve been on leave for two weeks now. My head was quickly filled with questions. I thanked the receptionist and made my way back to the elevator. Once I was headed back to the ground floor, I called Brook and asked her to pick me up. She verbally pinned me in a corner, agreeing to do so only if I would go to the doctors after. While I would have normally put up a stink, I was scared. I had apparently blacked out and then come to - disoriented and unaware of where I was. I knew it was time to get a diagnosis on this mystery illness.

It was the last days of June, and I tipped the scale at 210 pounds. I was wondering how much more weight I would end up putting on. When we got home from the elevator incident, Brook insisted that I immediately call the hospital and set up an appointment to get checked out. I obliged and got in touch with the local hospital. After relaying my symptoms and condition, we scheduled an appointment for the first of July, only three days away. I told Brook, and she called her boss to let her know she wouldn’t be in on that day. I was nervous because of what I had just gone through, but relieved that whatever it was I was experiencing, we were going to have answers very soon.

Brook Woodward

"Jeremy's physical change with the fluid was gradual, but to me, he looked and seemed miserable the minute he started putting on weight. But like anyone who knows Jeremy will tell you, he could be bleeding to death and he'd say he was fine. Even when he was having difficulty getting around on his own, he insisted that he was okay and that whatever was wrong would just run its course."

"There is this one vivid memory I have of one night in late June of that year. I had a friend in town that I hadn't seen in a while and we were going to meet up for dinner. I made Jeremy something small for dinner, which I knew he wouldn't eat. As I left, I looked back to Jeremy to say bye and saw that he was bent over the ottoman and clutching it tightly. At the time, since he was in an awful physical state all the time, I didn't think much of it. But in retrospect, I can't believe that we let it get that bad before going to the hospital."

The day came for my appointment. I went in with high hopes, expecting a quick diagnosis just like I had with the endocarditis several years ago. The thought of a heart-related condition had of course crossed my mind several times. But I was unsure because the symptoms with the endocarditis had come on quickly and severely, whereas this condition was the opposite, slow and not as debilitating. As I had become all too familiar with my annual echoes and checkups, I signed in and waited for my name to be called. When it was, I got a good luck kiss from Brook and followed the nurse back into the examining room. From the start, I could see that she was concerned once she saw my stomach and legs. I was told this was edema fluid and is common with injuries, such as breaks or fractures.

"But I haven't broken anything and it's on both legs and my stomach," I said. The nurse went on to explain that edema fluid can also occur with allergic reactions, liver disease, pregnancy and as a side effect from some medications. 'Oh darn, I need to check with Brook and make sure I'm not pregnant,' I thought, laughing to myself. The nurse listed several medications and asked if I was taking any of them. I was not. After running a few more tests and asking more questions, she asked if I could come back in two days for 'a couple of days' of observation. I agreed, set a date and time with the front desk, and left the hospital with a heavy heart. Brook and I had both gone in hoping for answers and left not only empty-handed, but with even more questions.

I checked back into the hospital on July 3rd, 2007, two days after my initial visit. History was repeating itself as I was hooked up to machines in an observation room and asked questions about how I felt. I spent the 4th of July in the hospital while my friends and family celebrated with each other, bummed out that I was missing being with them. But even if I wasn't in the hospital, I was in no shape to be socializing.

I endured three days of observation. Different staff members would come in every now and then, explain their different positions and run different tests. On July 7th, I was discharged from the hospital. Still I had no answers. The hospital staff told Brook and me that they were unsure of what was wrong. We were at a loss. The first visit had brought no answers, so they asked us to come back. I had just given them three days of full observation, and we still were left clueless. The hospital's advice? Go home, stay on home rest and come back in a month for follow-up observation. Brook and I left the hospital for a second time with no answers and feeling even more frustrated than before.

Home rest did nothing to ease my situation. My health continued to decline. I started having trouble walking and getting up from bed. My appetite also suffered. Bags formed under my eyes. I felt depressed. Each day felt like a month. I got fed up with trying to wait out a month, especially once I needed Brook's help just to move around our apartment. We decided to call Tufts Medical Center in Boston and make an appointment. They asked if I had any prior medical conditions. When I described the endocarditis from seven years ago, the idea of this being a heart-related condition popped back into my head. We made an appointment for July 21st. After hanging up, my wife and I both agreed we had just made the right decision. There was no way we could wait for an entire month.

Throughout the days leading up to our trips to Tufts, I was periodically on the phone with medical experts. It seemed they were asking me questions similar to what the staff at the local hospital had, but their questions seemed to be more specific. This was both alarming and reassuring. They seemed like they might know what was wrong: good. I would soon find out what was wrong: alarming.

The day before our trip to Tufts, I received a phone call from the hospital. I picked up, expecting more questions. This call was different. "Jeremy," the doctor started. "Based on your symptoms and prior medical history, we have determined what is ailing you. Your symptoms and physical condition all point to congestive heart failure." I was stunned. I put the phone on speaker mode so Brook could hear. The doctor added that he believed my condition had been brought about by deterioration of the tissue valve earlier than projected. I had been told that ten to fifteen years was what I could expect from the tissue valve. Seven years wasn't even at the bottom of the projection. "It was smart of you to not wait the month, based on your symptoms and current condition. This sounds like a serious case of congestive heart failure, and the worst stage of heart failure. We will be waiting for your arrival."

I couldn't speak. Brook thanked the doctor for us and ended the call. We spent several seconds looking at each other in silent shock. Her hands were covering her mouth. My eyes were wide in disbelief. We weren't prepared for that kind of news. Congestive heart failure. I couldn't wrap my head around that. As she choked back tears and tried to hold her emotions in check, Brook suggested that we pack an overnight bag. I tried to hold it together, but felt a hard lump forming in my throat from holding back tears of my own. A sniffle escaped as I leaned on Brook and hobbled into the bedroom to pack.

That night was rough, to say the least. We both wanted to talk about this new diagnosis, but neither of us could find the right words. A difficult silence filled the room. Every now and then one of us would throw in an attempt at a conversation starter, but the thoughts of what the future held, or may not hold, overshadowed any conversation. Also, I couldn't stop hearing the diagnosis from the doctor. *Congestive heart failure.* It kept popping into my head just when I'd gotten off of that trend of thought. I didn't get any sleep that night. My mind was running a mental marathon. I was physically drained. Night gave way to dawn and I decided to give up on sleep. I woke Brook up as I tried to get out of the bed to go to the bathroom. *Congestive heart failure.* I told her I had it and she could stay in bed, but there was no convincing her. Offering to help make breakfast was also out of the question. As I ate oatmeal (that was all I could handle that morning) I tried to savor it, knowing that this would be the last homemade meal I would have for a long while. Would I ever have another homemade meal? *Congestive heart failure.* These words had been dancing around my head all night. I had done some research during the night and seen some scary descriptions and statistics. I mentally steeled myself for whatever this visit to Boston might reveal.

Brook packed the car with the 'just-in-case you need this random thing from home' bag then helped me to the car. With a solemn air, she started the car and pulled up the directions on our GPS. Without a word we started our race to find a cure for my heart disease. As much as I wanted to lighten the mood with talk, I didn't have the energy and found myself staring out the window.

Rays of sunlight sliced through the partly cloudy sky, making me squint involuntarily. I marveled at the beauty. The beams of sunlight streaming down resembled massive scythes, cutting through the cotton-like clouds at abstract angles. The clouds themselves moved lazily across the endless blue, morphing constantly. Every now and then I was able to discern shapes and figures out of the clouds.

Though we are all exposed to these sights on a regular basis, I was looking at the horizon through a new set of eyes and with a new appreciation of my surroundings. The trees swaying ever so slightly in the breeze, the hawk coasting on the wind currents above, the feel of the midsummer warmth against my skin; all these sensory experiences seemed extraordinary at that time.

The date was July 21st, 2007. The UV index was 9, a high level even for summer in New England. However, the comfortable temperature of seventy degrees made the heat quite bearable. Despite the beautiful weather the mood was anything but cheery. We were driving to Tufts in order to learn how to treat what had been plaguing me for the past several months. My wife and I knew I was in the worst stage of heart failure. I was carrying forty pounds of excess fluid. As my wife drove I could feel her glancing worriedly at me from time to time. I couldn't bear to meet her gaze.

The clouds above which had previously seemed sluggish parted in haste, allowing sunlight to cascade through as if a faucet had just been thrown open. The suddenness forced my eyes shut even further. I fought through the urge to squint and stared up into the sky, wondering if I would soon be making a venture beyond the clouds and on into the heavens.

The hour-long drive from New Hampshire turned into almost three times that, although anyone that has driven in Boston can surely attest to having similar experiences. The pleasant summer air had given way to a muggy, almost damp feel to the atmosphere in downtown Boston. After multiple references to a street map and with a stroke of luck, we finally found the parking garage for Tufts. Brook accepted the stub at the ticket window and sped further into the garage. The first few rows of parking spots were completely full, as we expected. After she saw that the entire first floor was full, Brook hurriedly drove up to the second floor, only to see it too was packed. Even the third floor was full. Rather than go higher and make it a longer walk, she decided to circle back around and go back down to the lower floors.

That driving in the garage felt like an eternity. I was exhausted, drained of energy and devoid of emotion. My head was braced against the window at an uncomfortable angle that hurt my neck, but I was too tired to shift my position. Mercifully, after ten minutes that felt like a lifetime, we found a parking spot on the first level.

I glanced out the window in the direction of the entrance. I estimated we were about 100 yards from the doors. 'I can do this,' I thought to myself. 'Only a short walk and I'm good.' Brook came around to my side of the car, opened the door and helped me out of the car. I had to be careful where I placed my feet in order to avoid the litter - a root beer can, a plastic bag and several scraps of paper.

We were running late for my appointment. Brook had called the medical center on the drive down to tell them we were slightly behind schedule. I lifted my head and stared at the hospital doors. Though it was only 100 yards, the distance from the doors to where I stood seemed to be miles. With one hand on my arm and the other wrapped around me, Brook took a tentative step toward the doors, silently urging me forward. I grimaced and followed. A hundred yards is not a long distance for most people to walk. However, when one is dying of heart failure, has an empty stomach and is carrying forty pounds of excess fluid in their body, you'd better believe that walking any distance is a challenge in and of itself. Those hundred yards were the longest I have ever traveled in my life.

Every step was a chore. Every shuffle was excruciating. Every second was harder than the last. Sure, a wheelchair would have been much easier and faster, but anyone who knows me knows that I am far too stubborn to accept that kind of help. 'This is *my* life, *my* condition, *my* journey,' I thought to myself, and walking to that door without the aid of a wheelchair was something I needed to do on my own.

It must have taken a full ten minutes to walk from the car to those doors, and sensing my presence, they silently slid open. I had made it. I was at the medical center. The clean scent of the hospital wafted into my lungs. Now we could finally find out how to treat my condition. Taking a deep breath, I continued to put one foot in front of the other and entered the building, unaware that I was about to embark on the most unlikely journey of my life.

I knew that I shouldn't walk all the way through the hospital, so once I had successfully walked through the doors, I collapsed in one of the wheelchairs located just inside the hospital. I didn't like the idea, but knew that pushing myself further was not a smart move. Brook started wheeling me toward the cardiology office. As we moved down the hall, I smelled a café before it came into view. I asked Brook if we could stop in. She pointed out that we were already late for our appointment, but I countered with the point that I didn't know when my next meal would be. With an audible huff, my driver conceded.

The food smelled so good. As Brook walked back to the table with food, I saw that my nose was right: eggs and toast. My appetite had been off for the past three months, but I hadn't had any substantial food in days, so I dug in. The thought that this could be my last meal wandered into my head. 'Man, if that's the case, this sucks,' I thought, trying to lighten the mood with some dark humor. 'I was hoping for steak.'

I ate as much of the meal as I could before we headed up to the cardiology area. We checked in at the window and weren't even at the seating area before my name was called. Brook quickly pivoted the wheelchair in place and headed toward the open door and the waiting doctor as I gripped onto the armrests to keep from being ejected. The doctor greeted us and asked how I was feeling. "Not as good as I look," I joked. He did not respond to my quip as he led us into a side office.

Inside the office were three other medical staff members. They turned to face us as we entered the room. One introduced himself as the head cardiologist. He was my height, thin, with dark hair and glasses. We had been talking to him on the phone a lot but hadn't met. "Now that we're face to face, I'm amazed that you made it here in your condition," he remarked. His fellow staff all looked just as amazed as he did. "First we're going to check your vitals to see how much time we have before surgery," the cardiologist said as he moved a cart over to me. I knew this process too well after having it done so many times. I sat there and exchanged glances with Brook, trying to comfort her as the doctor started to poke and prod my neck area.

Right away, the cardiologist bluntly voiced his concerns.

"Jeremy, something's seriously wrong, more than I suspected earlier. Your numbers are way off. Even your pulse is raising red flags. We're almost all set with the lab, and then we'll go over what steps we will be taking." Two minutes later, they finished. The doctor took a large breath and let out a huge sigh, an obvious sign of distress that did not bode well for me. "Brook, Jeremy," he started. "It seems that your tissue valve is completely deteriorated, there seems to be nothing left. You're in the worst stage of heart failure; I'm honestly surprised you made it down here as you did." He took a deep breath and glanced down at his feet. I could tell he was about to drop a bombshell.

"Jeremy, we can't allow you to leave this hospital without at least a mechanical valve replacement, or possibly a heart transplant."

Brook Woodward

"Even though we had both known that heart failure was the problem, neither of us fully realized the scope of it until we got to Boston and the cardiologists gave us the run-down. It hit me when the doctors told us the news. I was in shock. I guess dealing with it for several months as a mystery condition and then confirming it was heart failure was what made me react as I did."

Brook broke down. I somehow managed to hold my composure. I had figured I'd require a valve replacement. The possibility that I may require a *heart transplant*, however, that was huge. Scary. I became completely numb, mentally and physically. I vaguely remember my wife leaning into me, but I didn't feel it at the time. My head felt like it had come to a complete block, as if I had just become a robot. Without thinking, I suggested:

"Could I go home and travel here daily for treatment?" The doctors literally gawked at me, looking back and forth between the head cardiologist and me.

"Jeremy, I don't think you're fully processing this right now, so let me put it bluntly. If you leave this hospital, I strongly believe that you will not make it back in alive."

Chapter Eight
Under the Knife...Again

After hearing those fateful words, I thought I'd be rushed into surgery. I was completely wrong. The doctors moved quickly to get me situated, but it was in a hospital room, not an operating room. While I was happy to be receiving treatment, I felt a slight sense of disdain at seeing the inside of a hospital room again. I was hoping that I wouldn't have to stay there for observation for a week, like I had for my initial tissue valve surgery. Well, my hopes came true: I didn't end up staying a week.

I ended up staying for much longer.

The doctors predicted that the surgery preparations would take two to four weeks. I was not happy about this at all, but I didn't have much time to dwell on it. I hadn't been in my room for five minutes before I received a dose of sedatives. I had just enough time to think 'Man, I hope these drugs kick in soon' before I blacked out.

I woke up in a fog. It took a few seconds to remember where I was. I struggled to sit up. The first thing I noticed was that I had dozens of wires, patches and tubes hooked up to me. I looked like the inside of a computer. Looking to either side of my bed showed that there were many more machines surrounding me than I expected. Some beeped in time with my heart, others occasionally flickered with lights, and others just sat there serving an unknown purpose. Even though I had slept for a long time (it looked to be morning outside) I felt as if I had only taken a cat nap. I was sore. I didn't feel any better than when I had been admitted, but I also didn't feel any worse. I took that as a good sign. I shifted myself back down in the bed and closed my eyes.

I slept almost the entire second day away. I woke up to a nurse taking readings and measurements from the machines. I mumbled a greeting to her, and she smiled in return. "Good afternoon! How are you feeling?" I sat up in bed, and to my surprise, I felt a lot less sore.

"Wow, I'm already feeling better!" I exclaimed. I felt around my legs and stomach and noticed that there was a notable decline in fluid. It wasn't a drastic change, but it was certainly a great start. A smile formed on my face for the first time in a long while. I turned and saw Brook sitting next to me, beaming in joy at the quick turnaround.

"Are you hungry?" the nurse asked. Again, to my pleasant surprise, I had a decent appetite.

"Yeah, I'd say so. Is it dinner time?"

"It's your call, late lunch or early dinner. Here, look at our menu and see what you think," the nurse suggested as she handed me a laminated sheet of paper. One side listed the breakfast and lunch options while the other side displayed the dinner and snack choices. I scanned through the lunch options and liked what I saw, but nothing stuck out as a good option at the time. I flipped the menu over and browsed the selection of dinner choices. My gaze settled on 'hospital chicken stir fry'. Reading the description made me salivate. I gave the rest of the items a once-over, but none sounded as good as the stir fry.

"Could I have the hospital chicken stir fry, please?"

"Absolutely. In the meantime, if you could take these along with some water, that would be great." She handed me a paper cup with several pills in it and a matching cup filled with water. I took both, tossing the pills back and chasing them with the water as the nurse walked out of the room, menu in hand. As she left, I turned to look at Brook. She smiled and took my hand.

"So you're feeling better?" she asked tentatively, squeezing my hand. I nodded my head in response, describing how I could feel that the fluid had already gone down a little bit. "The doctors have discussed surgery options with me, and I think that a mechanical valve implant is the smart decision," said my wife. She went on to explain the process, benefits and specifics involved. A mechanical valve would function more efficiently than a tissue valve would. Also, a mechanical valve would last almost three times as long as a tissue valve before requiring surgical maintenance. To further cement the decision, I wasn't keen on undergoing another tissue valve replacement with the experience I had just gone through, and an entire heart transplant seemed so cumbersome and intensive. After discussing logistics and other details, I agreed with Brook on a valve replacement. A mechanical valve would need more minute upkeep in the form of daily Coumadin intake to keep the valve clean, but the thirty-year comparison versus a tissue valve's life expectancy of ten to fifteen was what really helped make the decision for me.

Just as we finished discussing the surgery, the nurse returned to the room with a plate piled high with steaming food. My eyes fixated on the food that was fast approaching. It turned out that I was hungrier than I thought. The first bite of the stir fry tasted amazing. I almost let out a cry of joy at how good it was. After cleaning the plate Brook and I talked for another hour. She then kissed me goodbye and left for home, as she had to work the next morning.

Marshall Crane

"When I first heard that Jeremy was back in the hospital, I

dropped everything on the spot, grabbed my friend Billy and we booked it to Tufts. When we got there we were able to talk to Jeremy right away. He was telling us about the chances he had of survival when he initially walked into the hospital like he was telling us the weather. He had almost died and it seemed like it was nothing big to him. I questioned whether he'd be able to make a full recovery, he was in such rough shape."

"When we left, I was in shock for a bit. Once we got into the car, I started venting to Billy. Jeremy was the most fit and healthy person I knew, he didn't do any drugs or even drink. Why did this have to happen to him? It wasn't fair, and I was really upset about the whole situation. But I was pulling for Jeremy and a successful surgery."

Over the next week, I ordered the same meal for dinner every night. After several days, the nurse didn't even bother to bring in the menu for dinner. My only complaint in terms of food and drink was that I was very limited with my liquid intake. I was only allowed to have a small amount of liquid per day due to the built-up fluid in my legs and stomach. In addition, I was on a high dose of diuretics for the first ten days. Due to these diuretics, I was going to the bathroom an insane amount. I felt like my body was going to dry out like a sponge. Luckily, the only things that dried out were the concentrations of fluid in my legs and stomachs. Every day they looked and felt smaller than the previous day.

Unfortunately, I couldn't just get up out of my bed and go to the bathroom whenever I felt like it. I had to inform a hospital staff member that I needed 'a release'. They would then get a small, rounded tray and place it underneath me. Once I was all set, they took it away. This process repeated too many times to count each day. When I first started the diuretics, I felt like I was going to be pissing out gallons at a time. As the days passed and my fluid buildup shrank, so did my frequency of bathroom breaks. The diuretics were intense and lasted for ten days. I passed more fluid in those ten days than in a normal month, and was not upset when I was weaned off.

During this preparation time, Brook was my guardian angel. She was especially nurturing and caring through all of the tests. At least five days a week, she would take a bus from New Hampshire down to South Station in Boston and walk to Tufts from there. I could not have asked for a more supportive partner in this time.

I had lost a substantial amount of fluid from the diuretics, almost thirty pounds! "It looks like the hundreds of bathroom breaks have paid off," I joked to Brook one day. After the diuretics came pique lines. These are small lines that enter one's body through the neck and deliver antibiotics directly to the heart. I had these lines for five days after the diuretics. These were meant to ensure that my heart was healthy enough for surgery and as strong as possible. I was scheduled to have my surgery on August 3rd. On the 2nd, I received news that the head surgeon did not have access to his normal crew of supporting doctors and nurses, and the surgery was postponed for five days. I was completely okay with this; when it came to cutting open my body, taking things out and putting new things in, I wanted the person doing all of this to be as comfortable as possible. I amused my wife and several nurses with these comments. Heck, if the surgeon wanted me to be dressed like a clown for the surgery, I wouldn't have asked questions if it meant he was more comfortable.

During the days leading up to the surgery, I was left to my own devices: no diuretics or pique lines. It felt good to not have to worry about taking large doses of medicine or to be undergoing intense treatment. The day after the pique lines I woke up to a surprise: I had a roommate. I welcomed him to the hospital and we immediately started sharing stories. He introduced himself and told me he was a Boston firefighter. He explained that he had suffered a heart attack when fighting a large house fire. He was older than me, but still young. I didn't ask his age, but guessed that he was somewhere in his mid-thirties. He showed Brook and I pictures he had of his kids, two beautiful little girls. This amazing man was great at both providing conversations and excellent moral support. He talked about his job and the amazing stories that went along with it, and I talked about my racing background and how I hoped that would translate into a business someday. On the day before my surgery, he was cleared and discharged. We wished each other luck and embraced. I felt a tear building as I said goodbye. Even though I will probably never cross paths with that man again, I will never forget him for as long as I live.

The day before surgery I was daydreaming, thinking that I wanted to do something ground-breaking after recovery. Something that most people would think was impossible to do. I was browsing through a magazine to pass the time while Brook was making her way to the hospital from the train station. It was a sports magazine, the only one that could hold my attention out of the entire pile of magazines next to my bed. As I turned the page from an article on a football star, I came upon the centerfold spread of that issue. There was a collage of images of an athlete running, biking and swimming. 'Oh wow, he's a triathlete,' I thought to myself.

I read the short column stuffed onto the side of the page and learned that this athlete was a regular Ironman participant. The article went on to explain that the Ironman races are widely considered the most grueling and demanding single-day races. This guy regularly raced a 2.4-mile swim, a 112-mile bike ride and a full marathon, 26.2 miles. These numbers blew my mind; I think my jaw actually dropped when I read this. Any one of those three events is grueling and takes so much effort. Doing all three of them back-to-back, that was intense. I found myself inspired and motivated. I decided that if I could do (almost) a short triathlon with next to no time to prepare, I could certainly work my way to an Ironman race.

I had just finished reading the article for the third time when Brook walked in. I handed her the magazine and asked her to read the article. She did, and was just as impressed as I was. "Makes even the triathlon you competed in seem small, huh?"

"Yeah! Which is why after I'm recovered I'm going to train as much as I need to and do an Ironman race," I threw out matter-of-factly.

Brook stared at me as if I had grown a second head. She shifted in her chair, straightened up and cleared her throat. "Jeremy, I think before you go into surgery for your heart, you should call the doctor in and have him check the condition of your brain. An Ironman race? The race finishes with a marathon. *Finishes with a marathon.* That's after over a hundred miles on the bike and a massive swim. These racers must eat nails and grits for breakfast. That is insanity, you're nuts. Your goal should be to get out of the hospital. Anything that uses a marathon for one third of the entire race is ridiculous." I pointed out my slight success with the triathlon on short notice, but Brook stood her ground that an Ironman was a stretch.

"Just you watch. I'll ask the doctor when he comes in, and he'll tell you that I'll be able to do it!' My wife sighed and dropped the topic for the time being. When the doctor walked into the room several minutes later, I immediately called him over. "So doc, I want to do an Ironman race after I recover from surgery." I handed him the magazine article and asked him his opinion. He closed the magazine, set it back on the table and looked at me.

"Jeremy, I think you should get better first and dream later." That statement hurt. Brook gave me a knowing but sympathetic gaze accompanied by a faint smile. "Speaking of that, do you mind telling me what you normally do for physical activity?" I explained about my martial arts classes, my job as a fitness coach and my own personal training. After I was done and the doctor had taken in all of the information he gave me some news that I was not all too happy to hear.

"To be completely honest with you, I think you should seriously consider shelving at least your martial arts training. After this surgery, you will be on blood thinner medication for the rest of your life. Based on what you just described, the risks of serious injury or complications you would be running by continuing martial arts seems dangerous. Even the other physical activity seems aggressive for your position."

I set my jaw and nodded in silence. He could tell I was not pleased, and apologized. He left Brook and me alone in the room. I knew that openly defying the doctor to his face would have gotten me nowhere and only created unneeded tension. However, I also knew that voluntarily stopping martial arts was just as likely as voluntarily stopping breathing. Taking it slightly easier with the hard, heavy striking and sparring was an obvious move, but stopping was not an option. And as for the Ironman race, I had made a goal and made up my mind. I wanted to prove to my wife and the doctor that their scoffing and nay-saying was for naught.

That night Brook wished me luck, as I would be heading into surgery the following morning. She left early so that I could get plenty of rest. Just as with the endocarditis, I would be up in the wee hours of the morning and into surgery before most people are up for work. I closed my eyes that night knowing that the next day would bring about a totally different way of life for me.

On August 8th, two and a half weeks after bring admitted to Tufts for heart failure, I was prepared for open-heart surgery, as was the team of miracle workers that would be making the surgery happen. The early morning preparations went off without a hitch. As I was pushed through the halls, I caught glimpses of the morning sky. It wasn't much to look at: grey overcast clouds shrouded the horizon. The sun was trying to shine through, but the clouds refused to give way.

My heart was beating in anticipation as the large double doors to the operating room came into view. I had been preparing for this day for the past two weeks, and was determined to get through this. I looked at this as simply another challenge to overcome, another opponent to spar, another hill to climb. The lead surgeon had his team assembled and was ready to go the minute I was wheeled into the operating room. After shifting their tools around, I was given a sedative and asked to count to ten. I had only gotten to 'two' from my endocarditis, and I was determined to top that performance. I pushed through and barely mustered a weak 'four' before slipping into unconsciousness.

Part Three – A New Lease on Life

Chapter Nine
The First Steps to a New Foundation

I started drifting back into consciousness. I heard muffled sounds here and there. They sounded like voices, but I wasn't sure. Something was beeping every now and then. Next came some feeling - it felt like there was a tube in my throat, I moved my head and felt the sensation of a soft pillow. I was able to move my left hand and sensed that I had lots of cords and wires attached to me. I couldn't smell anything, and breathing hurt. Someone was removing things from my arm. Beeps, clicks and a bunch of other mechanical sounds were flooding my ears. While this was a lot for my senses, they were all sounds of life, they meant that I had made it through. I heard what I thought was 'he's coming back' from one of the staff as I opened my eyes slightly, trying to adjust to the light in the room.

I was covered with wires, even more than in the weeks leading up to surgery. I could see wires of all colors attached to a multitude of machines. Without warning, a lance of pain shot up through my left side. I winced and let out a gasp of air as my hand involuntarily clutched at my ribs. It was a white-hot pain that left as soon as it came. I let my hand drop slowly back to my side. No sooner had my hand come to a rest then the pain rushed right back, this time worse than before, a burning pain that I have a hard time putting fully into words. This process cycled through several times before I made eye contact with a nurse. I pointed to my side. I couldn't speak because of the tube, and even if I could, the pain only allowed for very shallow breaths.

"You suffered a collapsed lung during surgery. We needed an extra two hours for the surgery because of it. Try not to take any deep breaths for now. The medication will also help with the pain." I nodded in acknowledgement and the nurse gave me a sympathetic smile. I laid my head back down and tried to ignore the incredible degree of pain I was in. My side felt like I had been hit repeatedly with a baseball bat.

I was kept in the ICU for 48 hours following surgery, which is the standard procedure for situations like mine. I slowly regained my motor functions during this time. I could tell that my face was swollen, especially my lips. Once the doctors decided that I was stable, my family was allowed to come and see me. I almost cried in relief when Brook came in the room the night after my surgery. I wanted to jump out of the bed and hug her. Since I couldn't even sit up in bed, that action was out of the question. The tube had just been removed from my throat, but I could barely talk. I was able to give one-word responses, which was better than nothing. We were both just overjoyed to see each other and be in each other's company. She looked surprised at my physical state and commented on the condition of my face, pointing out that I looked like I had been attacked by bees.

She never left my side as the rest of my family filed in bit by bit. My parents came in to see me, then Brook's mother, followed by my brothers and several cousins. I was already drained from the surgery, and all the family interaction made me even more exhausted. After talking with my wife for a little longer, I was about ready to pass out. She kissed my forehead and wished me a good night's sleep. She hadn't even left the room before I was out.

The next morning I woke up and immediately vomited, just barely grabbing the bin next to my bed in time. I scared the nurse that had been cleaning my room. After spitting out the last remnants, I nodded at the nurse and managed a raspy 'sorry'. She said that the throwing up was probably a side effect from the anesthesia I had received for the surgery and that almost every patient in my position does the same thing. She offered me some watered down apple juice to see if my stomach could handle it. I accepted it and took a large sip, as I was parched from not having anything to eat or drink for over a day. As luck would have it, my stomach refused to cooperate and I threw up again. "We'll try some soft foods in about a half hour," the nurse muttered as she took the bucket from me.

To my surprise, she walked back in a half hour later with ice cream. I was overjoyed. Not that hospital food wasn't good (I planned to order hospital stir fry that night), but ice cream? I felt spoiled as she handed it to me. Thankfully, I was able to keep it down. Just as I finished the ice cream, she offered me a popsicle. My eyes widened. I couldn't believe it. I felt like I was cheating on a healthy diet right now, and I was being encouraged to do so by the hospital staff. I was amused at the irony as I bit into the fruit-flavored treat. I was able to get through half of it before my stomach warned me that I was pushing it. Rather than risk throwing up the sugary goodness, I tossed the rest of it.

Now that I was stable and into the recovery process, the doctors were able to discuss the details of the procedure with Brook and me. The surgery had been successful. They had removed what was left of the deteriorated tissue valve and put in a mechanical valve. While this type of valve would not deteriorate as the tissue valve had and would last exponentially longer, it would require a degree of maintenance that the tissue valve had not. The doctors explained that I would need to take a drug called Coumadin daily. And this wasn't just until I was back in shape, this was for the rest of my life. At first that sounded very daunting, but he explained that it was easy to manage and not a hassle.

He also explained the issue of my collapsed lung during surgery. The six-hour surgery had taken eight hours because of that added problem. The staff had also had to keep the tube in my throat longer and monitor me more closely immediately after the surgery. But overall, I was healing up nicely and off to a good start on my road to recovery. After he finished going over the details of the procedure and we asked several questions, he said, "Okay Jeremy, let's get you up and test out your legs."

"Uh, wait, ha, what?" I stuttered. I felt better, but had a hard time transitioning from lying down to sitting up. "Walking? Right now?"

"Are you up for it?" The doctor questioned.

I grimaced and uttered a 'sure' as I sat up in the bed. He wheeled a walker over to my bedside. The doctor then unhooked a majority of the wires and patches from my body, leaving only a few that were attached to a mobile machine. As he was unplugging me, I gripped the hard plastic tip of the handles to the walker, shifting them around to test the grip and hold of the legs against the floor. "Alright, come on up. Easy does it," the doctor coached. This was an odd change in roles. I was used to training and assisting others, and now I was on the receiving end of the coaching. I grunted with effort as I pushed myself up. The doctor braced me as I stood up as straight as I could. I grasped for the handles of the walker to steady myself. Brook was on one side of me, the doctor on the other. My legs could barely hold my weight, and I had to lean on the walker to avoid collapsing, my knuckles white with effort. I let out a gasp. My doctor asked if I wanted to wait until later, but I refused.

Brook went to open the door as I shuffled my way across the room. Once I passed through the doorway I asked the doctor through gritted teeth where I was going. "We're going to do a lap around the ICU today to see how you feel," he replied. The walk to the door had been rough enough. Not as bad as when I had the fluid weight, but I was still struggling. I turned to the right and started my trek around the floor. I switched between leaning on the walker and my doctor for support. Brook offered to help, but of course I was too proud to accept it.

The area that I was doing the lap couldn't have been more than 150 feet or so. It was the perimeter of the large nursing station in the center of the floor. At first glance, it looks so easy. A little bit over thirty feet per length of the square walls. That's probably thirty or so shuffles per side, I thought as I broke it down. I put my chin down and kept going. Whenever a nurse and I made eye contact, they would flash me a sympathetic smile or a knowing head nod.

After pushing myself to the limit, I was making my way back into my room. I rushed to flop back down on the bed. My doctor congratulated me on my performance. "It may not seem like that much of an accomplishment, but I've never seen someone use as little assistance on their first lap as you did today. Keep up that pace and you'll recover in no time! We'll try two laps tomorrow. Until then, get some well-earned rest and relaxation." As he left, he did something I hadn't seen him do yet in my time there: he smiled.

I thanked the doctor as he left the room. Brook congratulated me on my performance, beaming at my efforts. She had to work early the next morning and needed some rest of her own. When she left the room my eyes came to rest on the magazine pile next to my bed. I decided to give it a shot, but didn't have very high expectations. As luck would have it, a sports magazine was hidden in the middle of the pile, the same one as I had been reading earlier. I flipped open the magazine to see the familiar centerfold of the Ironman athlete. I daydreamed the rest of the day away, with a quick break to fit in a small helping of stir fry.

Two days later I was cleared from the intensive care unit and moved to a transition room. I was still on the same floor of the hospital, but off of the ICU wing of the floor. A day later I stopped using a walker during my daily laps. I was matching my amount of laps with the day. On my fourth day of recovery, I completed four laps, the fifth day five laps, and so on. I felt better with every passing day. I was given an extraordinary amount of freedom during this time. I passed time by reading books, watching TV and talking with other patients on the floor. Hearing some of the other patients' experiences and stories helped to put my own experience in perspective. While most of my fellow patients were recovering from mild conditions, others had suffered horrible setbacks. No matter what the ailment, everyone was so positive and optimistic; it was contagious.

At one point when I only had several days left in the hospital before being released, Brook and I were having an in-depth talk about our futures. At a pause in the conversation, I took a moment to just admire her. Her hair looked perfect that day. Her eyes were sparkling. The sun coming in through the window only made her glow brighter. "You know," I started. "The doctor just checked me out, so he'll be gone for a while. The door is closed, the windows are covered, and we haven't had any…quality alone time in a while," I said with a smirk and a wink. Brook blushed and chuckled.

"Jeremy, we're in a hospital. It's the middle of the afternoon! And no offense, but that johnny doesn't exactly show off your figure all that well," she joked. I knew I wouldn't get anywhere, but it was worth a shot.

One day, after completing my 20th lap around the floor I made my way back into my room. A nurse was fiddling with one of the machines in the room and greeted me as I walked in. It was almost lunchtime, so I picked up the menu to see what looked appealing.

"Excuse me. I don't think you'll need that, Jeremy. You've been cleared to leave. We called Brook and she is on her way to pick you up." I was surprised at the news, and just as excited about it. I certainly wasn't back to one hundred percent, I was still far from it. But I was recovering nicely. Having no fluid weight to carry around felt amazing, and I was anxious to get home and finish my recovery so I could get back into the swing of things.

Brook picked me up right around dinner time. Even though I was hungry, I was willing to wait for a meal in my own kitchen with my own utensils. The ride back up to New Hampshire was pleasant. Brook and I talked mostly about the timeline I would be working with, when I would go back to work, what would be easiest, what would be a challenge and everything in between.

That night, I stepped out of Brook's car and looked at a sight I hadn't seen in a month: our apartment building. I smiled from ear to ear. "It's great to be home," I commented to Brook.

"It's great to have you back home," she answered as she kissed my cheek. When I had last left that apartment building, I couldn't walk down the steps on my own. Now I bounded up them with bags in hand. It felt great to be home.

I was on home rest for just as long as I had been for the endocarditis. I was expected to remain on home rest for a total of six weeks. I had lots of down time and to be honest, I embraced it. Taking a nap every day was great. I had always been one to be running around between work and social events and more work, so to be able to wind down was a nice change. I finally was cleared to go back to work in the middle of October of 2007, months since I had taken my leave from my job. The week before I was fully cleared, I called all of my previous clients to inform them that I was coming back to work. To my pleasant surprise, most of them were exceptionally pleased to hear the news.

It was bittersweet to get back to work at the gym. Seeing all of my old clients again was great, and the occasional new client was just as rewarding as always. On the other hand, getting out of the lazy mode I had slipped into during recovery was difficult. During my first week back, I felt exceptionally tired after work, even with a short twenty-hour work week. Having to transfer from long naps and lounging around with only my thoughts to keep me busy was a stark contrast to being a physical fitness trainer. I had to make sure that I transitioned slowly in order to not run myself into the ground. Four weeks passed before I was able to get back into the full swing of work.

During those four weeks, I did a lot of reflecting on the path I had taken in life up to this point. In truth, I almost didn't go back into fitness training for work. I knew that I couldn't get back into peak shape by just waiting a month. Training and a lot of effort would be required to get back to the top form I had been in before heart failure. Not only that, but there is a mindset that comes with being a fitness trainer, and just like muscles, dissipates if not actively maintained. After lots of wrestling with my own thoughts, I decided that the end result of getting back to where I had been was worth the effort and time. I set new goals. I had been given a new lease on life - literally. I wanted to make the most of this second chance.

In order to stay on top of my condition, Tufts Medical Center enrolled me in a cardiac rehabilitation program through Concord Hospital. The goal of this program was to monitor heart activity and stability during workouts and other stress-related conditions. Mostly, the idea was to make sure my heart rate didn't spike out of control due to any unseen complications. The first class was pretty eye-opening. Every other rehabilitation patient looked to be at least in their sixties to seventies. I was by far the youngest member of the program. This told me that I needed to be even more in tune with my maintenance of my condition.

Through close monitoring and self-pacing, I got stronger and stronger. By the time the first snowflakes of winter came falling down, I was almost at full strength. It was at this time that Brook and I started seriously contemplating the idea of starting a family. We both had steady jobs and we had our own place. After the events in the recent past I realized that life, however long it ends up being, is too short. We both wanted kids, so it felt only natural that we start planning out the next chapter of our lives. One day at the end of January, I came home from work and was undergoing my usual routine: keys on the table, shoes off at the door, belt undone, and big stretch. In the middle of my routine, my wife rushed out of the bathroom and approached me at the door, doing a terrible job of hiding a smile. When I asked her what was going on, she replied with the announcement that we were going to be getting a new member in our family.

I was going to be a father. I had been looking forward to this moment for a long time. I was on top of the world and nothing could bring me down. I remember picking Brook up and twirling her around in the air in reaction to the news.

We immediately embraced the idea of parenting and started brainstorming potential names. Once we found out we were having a girl, Brook and I started narrowing down the name possibilities. We both wanted something unique. I suggested Kona, the name of the city that hosted the Ironman World Championships. However, Brook was apprehensive with the suggestion. She then went out and bought an overpriced book that was simply a list of baby names with a cover and binding. "Hun, what do you think about Elliana?" she said one night during dinner. I let it sit for a few seconds before answering.

"You know what? I actually really like that!" And it was easy as that. We decided on Elliana for our daughter's first name with Kona as her middle name.

That summer, we moved from one apartment to a bigger one across town in order to make room for the fast-approaching addition to our family. The summer of 2008 also brought another big event: I tested for my fourth degree black belt. The black belt tests are normally held on the last weekend of June, but despite my protests, Mr. Hardy wouldn't allow me to test in June, citing my need to recover and catch up on the material and time that I had missed the previous year.

As much I was unwilling to admit it, Mr. Hardy was on point. I had been nervous just to get back into training because of what the doctors had told me regarding my martial arts training. In Combined Kenpo, we run choreographed sets of moves to address certain entries, be it a punch, kick, multiple strikes, weapon, etc. These sets are often very complex, and at the upper levels of the system, we 'blend' from one set to another. Because of the hard, contact-oriented nature of our system, I had plenty of worries about my safety. What if I slipped and my partner misplaced a strike because of it? What if my partner lost control and hit too hard on a certain strike? What if I passed out? With the Coumadin, I could have a devastating accident from a simple mistake due to the blood thinning. I could get injured far easier than anyone else in the school. Also, I had to think about more than just myself and Brook now. With a child on the way, I was forced to assess my situation and ask myself if I was being reckless.

Because of these variables, my test was pushed back to August, where I tested with another student that had suffered a construction accident and lost part of his thumb in June. The two of us underwent a grueling 12-hour day in the middle of a hayfield with just our headmaster as an audience. While the work was harder than ever because of the small size, Mr. Hardy was able to keep a close eye on me in case I started showing signs of fading or I started getting too big for my britches. We were tested in every way possible. We ran weapon forms, empty hand forms, techniques, line work, basics, drills to address random attacks, and so much more. After I was pushed to my physical and mental limit, I passed the test and earned my fourth degree black belt in Combined Kenpo.

Mr. Hardy

"Before Jeremy went in for his open-heart surgery, I clearly remember seeing him with the excess fluid weight. Honestly, it was really scary to see. The entire school was in shock. Jeremy was, and still is, one of our highest ranking members, so seeing him in that condition was difficult for everyone. I knew Jeremy was tough, but I really wasn't sure if I'd ever see him in the dojo as a student again; that's how bad it was."

"But as usual, Jeremy dominated the obstacles that he faced. He has never had anything but the utmost toughness. Even post-surgery, Jeremy will never take the easy way out, ever. He trains in martial arts like there might not be a tomorrow. That's what impresses me the most."

"When he tested in August for his fourth degree, I tried to get him to hold back and take it easy. But as I expected, he did all but that. He didn't back down from any drill or degree of physical striking. I think that because of what he has been through, Jeremy approaches martial arts as none of us could ever understand. He lives the promise he made to himself every day, the promise that he wouldn't let his past dictate his future. As a matter of fact, his commitment to martial arts has only strengthened since his surgery. To me, that is the best anyone could ask for."

Just as I was asking myself questions about my martial arts training, I started to do the same with my training for triathlons. I asked myself why I was doing this. Why was I training so hard for something I had only done once, and had done on a dare? The answer that came to me surprised me. Without thinking, I realized that I was working this hard because of the promise I had made to myself in the hospital. I had started my own race to become an Ironman, and I needed to continue this race to its finish. And while this, like martial arts, was a risk because of my heart condition, it was certainly a risk I was willing to take.

At the end of that summer, I was contacted by one of my friends who had raced in Ironman competitions. He had competed in the previous year and said that he was competing in an Ironman race in New York in two weeks. "I have VIP tickets for the race that you could have. You'd be right in the middle of the action." I loved the idea, and once I saw that I had no work on that weekend, I made plans to head out to New York for the weekend.

Watching my first Ironman race was eye-opening. Triathlons were one thing, but an Ironman was a whole different world. After being around that environment with the crowd and racers for just a few hours, I was hooked. My longing to race in an Ironman burned stronger after watching that year. I talked to my friend after the race and decided to volunteer at the same race in 2009.

As the summer of 2008 drew to a close, Elliana, our daughter, was fast approaching. She was due around the last days of September. The first Saturday of September, Brook and I had plans to go to a birthing class. As we were about to head out, Brook's water broke. Ellie was coming almost three weeks early! We rushed to the hospital, both of us a bundle of emotions. Once Brook was checked in and situated, we were able to breathe a sigh of relief. All of Saturday and Sunday were mostly uneventful. It was odd to be on the other end of things in a hospital; every other time, Brook had been the one holding my hand as I was confined to a bed. This time, I was supporting her.

Then came Monday, September 8th, 2008. Brook had gone into labor early in the evening on Sunday. I didn't know what to feel during this time. One minute I was freaking out with anxiety, the next

I was beaming, the next I was a mess of nerves. Just after midnight Elliana Kona Woodward was born. I wish I could describe my feelings in those first moments of fatherhood. The best way I can think to describe is a feeling of pride and excitement so strong that my chest felt tight; unconditional, instantaneous love. I remember crying in joy with Brook at our little bundle of love. Seeing Elliana's little fingers and how perfect she was is one of the best moments in my life to this day.

Having a daughter taught me many things (mainly that the amount of stink that can come from such a little diaper is unreal) and has certainly changed my life. Having a newborn was a drastic lifestyle change. Just getting into the groove of everything that is involved is hard, as it comes on so abruptly. The late nights tending to her were bittersweet; I always liked caring for her when she woke up in the middle of the night crying, but the sleep deprivation took its toll. A few months into parenthood, Brook and I knew that we needed more room to raise our daughter and started planning for an eventual move into a bigger space. Our lives were coming together as a family. I look back on this time in our lives with a warm heart and an ear-to-ear smile.

Chapter Ten
The Turning Point

Fast forward to the summer of 2009 and I was back in New York to volunteer at Ironman: Lake Placid. The forecast for the race was looking rough, calling for torrential rains. I was so excited for this race. Lots of friends raced that day, several of them for their first Ironman race. I was also going to be volunteering with friends. All in all, I was looking forward to the entire experience and couldn't wait.

The morning of race day saw us up at five in the morning. My friends and I showered and ate a good breakfast. Friends who were competing had already woken up and were warming up for the excruciating day they had ahead of them. Once my friends were all set, we left the hotel room and headed down to the docks where the race would be starting.

Sure enough, the forecast had been dead on: the rain was coming down so hard that puddles were already forming on the roadways. Cars were traveling cautiously, and brake lights could be seen everywhere. We had planned ahead and were equipped with rain coats and other gear to help keep us as dry as possible. We got down to the docks to a scene that will stick with me forever. We were up close with all of the athletes. Just the air they had about them was different than I was used to. The area was teeming with energy and noise from the massive amount of racers. I knew that any one of these individuals could crush the triathlon I had attempted two years ago. I smirked at the thought that the triathlon I had tried would serve as a warm-up for these competitors. Just as I had observed during my triathlon, most of the competitors were walking into the water for several moments, standing still, and then making their way back out without so much as a word or look to anyone during this process, reminding me of the same scene from my race, along with what it symbolized.

The rain was making for quite a sight on the surface of the lake. The usually smooth water was rippling constantly. It looked almost like the surface of the lake was vibrating because of the amount of rain. This was the kind of rain that feels heavy after a while. I couldn't imagine racing in this weather. I was having a hard enough time dealing with it just standing there, and these competitors were about to race almost 150 miles! I shook my head in disbelief. As I did, rain poured off the sides of my hood.

My friends and I were gathered together at the docks with a crew of volunteers and one of the racers. The racer's name was Michael, and according to what I had heard, he was an Ironman legend and one of the competitors for the fastest time in the race that day. He and a lead volunteer corralled several of us that had been assigned to work with him. There looked to be about eight or ten in my group. He went over the technique to use for handing off water bottles. It actually wasn't as simple and self-explanatory as I would have thought. After his explanation, it made complete sense. With athletes traveling 25-30 miles per hour on their bikes, volunteers had to be right on with our handoff technique, similar to handing off a baton in an interval race. Otherwise, we could mess up the entire race for these competitors.

We all huddled together for the start of the race. An announcer came over the speakers and announced some general information. The race would be starting promptly at 7:00; my watch read 6:55. The announcer then described the race. It would start with a 2.4-mile swim, followed by a 112-mile bike ride and end with a 26.2 mile marathon. There were also cutoff times for each leg of the race. The swim would be cut off at 9:20 a.m., the bike ride would be cut off at 5:20 p.m., and the entire race cut off was midnight. I was amazed at these numbers. Even though I had known the distances and times beforehand, seeing all of these elite athletes prepared to make all of the cut offs was astounding.

The one-minute warning came over the speakers and the racers filed into place on the shore of the lake. For several moments, all you could hear was the patter of the falling rain against the water, docks and wetsuits. I looked across the field of racers. Every single one looked to be in the zone, poised to plunge into the lake at the sound of the start. Sure enough, the racers took off like a shot at the sound of the starting gun.

The water foamed white from the thrashing bodies suddenly cutting through the surface. The combination of all the arms slicing through the water created a sound like distant thunder. If someone hadn't seen the racers, they would have thought that this was an active thunderstorm instead of just rain. Red and white swimming caps covered the surface of the water. It was appalling to see the sheer amount of participants in the water. Seeing these elite athletes starting the first strokes of a 2.4-mile swim was very inspiring. The next 17 hours would have these amazing individuals putting themselves through some of the most physically demanding situations found anywhere on this planet. After seeing the start, I now wanted to strive for my first Ironman even more.

Once all of the racers had started and were well on their way into the swim, shuttles drove down to the dock to move the volunteers to the other areas of the course. I would mainly be assisting on the bike course with the water aid station. The ride from the docks to the aid station was about fifteen miles by shuttle. On the way, the lead volunteer for our group reviewed the guidelines and techniques Michael had introduced to us.

When we got to the aid station, we were told to gather under the main canopy that was set up on the side of the road. All of the volunteers fast-walked to get out from the constant pounding rain for the first time that morning. Wind started to accompany the rain, making conditions even more brutal. Puddles were combining into mini ponds forming across the road, creating another hazard for the competitors to cope with. We were told to be prepared for racers to start filtering through in roughly five minutes. I did the math quickly in my head, and this suggested that the elite of the elite were going to be finishing the 2.4-mile swim on either side of an hour. This was an insane speed. I couldn't believe it! These people were the real deal, and I was thrilled at the idea of competing alongside them soon.

Sure enough, the first racer emerged onto the road at just shy of an hour after the start of the race. A team of volunteers that were assigned to that racer got into their respective positions. As the racer rode by, volunteers started working together like a well-oiled machine and handed off water bottles to him at two different points. I saw that we were going to be getting up close and personal with the racers and the course. This one racer, being one of the top competitors of the day, grabbed the bottles with no loss of speed and rode off into the distance. There were several chemical toilets scattered across the side of the road for volunteers and racers alike, although I was told none of the first racers would be stopping at these. I knew that they were trying for the fastest times of the day, so I asked the lead volunteer a question that started to bug me.

"What do the top racers do about going to the bathroom during the race if they don't stop?"

Without missing a beat, the lead volunteer matter-of-factly answered,

"They just go while racing. They don't have many, if any, solid foods while racing, so they don't have to worry about that. And so that they don't have to stop and tack on valuable time, they just go as they race." I had thought that might have been the answer, but was still shocked to find out that was actually the case. Just as he finished his explanation, I was told to get ready for the water bottle handoff for Michael.

The process went off without any issues. It was so much fun. We also kept helping at the station with maintenance and cleanup after Michael cruised by. It was interesting to see the racers pass by; at some points there was just one or two here and there, and other times it was crowded and chaotic because of the number of bikes flying by. The ebb and flow of racers kept us on our toes throughout the day. I was busy the entire time at the aid station and there was never a dull moment.

As much fun as it was to be assisting at the aid station, some of the experience was unnerving. From time to time we saw racers being carried into the medical tent that was set up next to our aid tent. Occasionally, these racers were loaded into an ambulance and transported away to treat hypothermia from the cold rain. The rain made the conditions terrible for the racers; even after finishing a cold swim, the rain was relentless on a bike. The 25-30 mph speed of the bike ride added to the freezing effect of the precipitation. I felt for these athletes. They came to this city with the intent of running across the finish line of the world's hardest race, and instead they were being rolled into the back of an ambulance.

To my surprise, some volunteers started cleaning up the aid stations even as some racers were still riding by. I asked one of my fellow volunteers that had done this before why they were cleaning up already. "Even though the cut off is still a ways off, they'll pick up racers that are obviously not going to make the cut off of that leg of the race," the volunteer explained. I looked at my watch and saw that it wasn't even close to the cut off time for the bike leg of the race.

What the volunteer had said made sense. If a racer barely made the swimming cutoff and started to lag behind on the riding leg of the race, it made sense for those racers to be picked up. In fact, just as our aid station was being cleaned up I saw volunteers riding next to a competitor and talking to him. He was almost screaming and was clearly upset. Just as he passed me, he dismounted his bike and got onto the shuttle with his bike in his hand. It looked like he was crying as he shook his head from side to side in disappointment. I can't say that I faulted him for that. Knowing how much work I would need to undergo to be able to complete an Ironman race, I'm sure I would react similarly if I met the same fate.

We finished cleaning up the rest of our station and packed up the aid tents and canopies about an hour before the riding cut off. Once that was done, the volunteers got another shuttle ride to the end of the race, where we could relax and watch the racers as they crossed the finish line. Even though the race still had over five hours before it ended, the finish line was much busier than the beach had been in the morning. The area was packed. And I don't just mean 'slightly crowded' packed, I mean 'standing close together like the pit of a popular concert' packed. There was music pumping through the speakers as racers crossed the finish line. They all reacted differently to crossing under the Ironman dome that was erected over the finish line, but all of their reactions were ones of pure joy. As each racer passed under the dome, the announcer's voice overrode the music and boomed "*you are an Ironman*". I knew that one day, I would be hearing that voice again, but it would be as I ran under the dome myself, and hopefully with better weather conditions.

Watching each of the racers cross the finish line got me thinking. I had gone through so many experiences to get where I was at that point, and I wasn't showing any signs of slowing down. Each person that finished the Ironman race had their own unique stories, their own hardships and their own unique paths through life that had led them to this point. Seeing these hundreds of unique stories running to Ironman-hood made me yearn for my opportunity even more.

As day turned to night, the top finishers of the Ironman race had passed through and the main body of racers was coming across the finish line. My friends that I had volunteered with that day went especially crazy with applause when our competing friends crossed the finish line with their arms raised in triumph. Before we knew it, the race came to a close at midnight. Our group of friends made our way back to the hotel rooms to celebrate and reflect on the day. We didn't head to bed, however, because in the wee hours of the morning we made our way back to the race area to sign up for next year's Ironman race at the same venue. The signups for an Ironman race start in the early morning hours immediately following the previous year's race. According to friends that had competed before, signups were completely filled for a future race within 12 hours following the finish of a race. I made the commitment and signed myself up for Ironman: Lake Placid 2010. I had already been working toward finishing an Ironman, and now I had a deadline. I had 365 days to train for the race of my life.

Chapter Eleven
The Calm Before the Storm

After watching and volunteering at Ironman, I started increasing my training so that I'd be able to compete myself. At first I was a little bit flustered. I knew what I had to do to train, I just didn't know how much per event or for how long. Should I do a one hour ride or a six hour ride after a ten mile run? What percentage of time should I devote to practicing swimming? Overall, how long should I be training per week? I had so many questions at first and didn't know where to find the answers, so I just did what felt right. Later, I established an organized schedule in order to best prepare for my ultimate goal.

I also sought out a coach for my Ironman training. I had been following a guy named Sean Snow for a while and wanted to work with him for some time, as he was an Ironman athlete himself. He was a respected and well-known coach. I contacted him and went over my plan and timeline, and he agreed to work with me. At first he was nervous at taking the risk of training me due to my heart condition, but in the end he obliged.

He designed most of my workout plans and quickly learned my limits. He re-designed those plans about a month in to push me to the endurance and made me a better athlete overall.

When I got into the zone in training, I had a lot of time with just my thoughts. when I got into the zone in training, I had a lot of time with just my thoughts. With time-consuming training sessions, I would often play games as I ran, mostly counting related. Counting the cars that passed, the street signs I flew by, and even animals I saw. Whenever I grew bored with these number games, I would visualize my martial arts forms in my head. Even though I'd be running or biking or swimming, I was thinking about a certain section of a form and how it applied to a technique. Mentally running the sequences of moves that made up the forms in our system was both stimulating and an excellent way to pass the time as I trained so my mind didn't wander. If I allowed my mind to wander, it would always end up settling on the fatigue I was feeling from training, making my work out that much more difficult.

Brook Woodward

"Jeremy was excellent at planning his training around family events and plans. Even if he did have to miss something, he was always great about making up for it at a later time. Sometimes after training sessions, he would come back for family time and be drained, which I wasn't always pleased about. Between training and planning for Ironman, fundraising updates and everything else, there was lot to keep track of. I felt overwhelmed at times, and I wasn't even in the thick of it. On a side note, the grocery bill skyrocketed in the months leading up to Ironman."

I also thought about my job and business oriented topics, especially when I rode my bike. I joke with my friends that my time on the bike during training is my most productive time of the day, and when I come up with my most creative and best ideas. On one of these rides, I was trying to come up with some cool ideas for something to make my Ironman race connect to something local. I had almost given up when my thoughts drifted to my work schedule at the gym later that day. It was then that I thought of a wonderful idea that I would pursue that night at work.

One of my clients that night, Daryl, was the director of the Nature Conservancy in New Hampshire. At the end of his class, we were catching up, having a light conversation. I then decided to tell him what I had been thinking about that day. I told him that I wanted to do some fundraising in conjunction with my race. Sometimes Ironman athletes don't fundraise for a cause, but I wanted to make a difference. Daryl suggested that I could work with the Nature Conservancy and get an entire campaign going for fundraising. I loved the idea and was happy that he was on board, and I told him I was looking forward to working on this. "Me too, Jeremy. Let's do something different, an idea that's never been done before." We worked out some small details at that point. The next day, he contacted me and informed me that he had set a date for me to meet with the Board of Trustees of the Nature Conservancy.

The meeting went better than I could have hoped. All of the board members were extremely supportive. The board members also had excellent ideas of their own. One of the board members presented the interesting concept that I advertise the goal of raising one thousand dollars for every mile of the Ironman. I quickly did the math in my head and came up with a giant number. If successful, that would mean I would raise over 140,000 dollars before it was all said and done! It was certainly possible if done correctly, but I would need a strong backing the whole way. As it turned out, the Board of Trustees had ideas for a successful strategy as well.

They suggested that we reach out to the Governor's office and ask to use the state house entrance on Main Street to announce our campaign.

It seemed like a great plan, and was certain to generate plenty of local buzz if executed properly. The next day the conference call was made to the Governor's office. After explaining who we were and what our goal was, including the concept of $1,000 of fundraising for each mile of the race, we were put on hold for a minute. I was nervous throughout that heavy silence.

When the secretary came back from hold, they had a counter offer. "I just spoke briefly with Governor Lynch, and we have an alternative proposal. Rather than simply announce it in front of the state house, the governor would like to back you with his full support for the duration of your campaign." I was astounded. The Board of Trustees and I looked around at each other in pleasant surprise. The Governor wanted to support me in my efforts. This was unreal. Daryl replied and said that sounded great. Plans were made to iron out the specifics of the presentation and fundraising efforts and the call ended. I was congratulated all around by the board members. They were all genuinely happy and thankful about this, and I was no different.

On November 19th, I gave a speech on the front lawn of the state house to a large crowd of onlookers, supporters and press. Governor Lynch stood beside me through the entire speech to show his support. He also gave a short speech pushing support for my cause. This speech and the fundraising campaign were featured in numerous local papers and news reports. Donations started flooding in. I was excited to be supporting a great cause and to have the backing of the community.

At this time, my training started to kick into high gear. Intensive training sessions, eating plans and strict attention to detail became a part of my everyday life. I realized that this is a selfish sport that I was a part of. I often had to sacrifice time with Brook and Ellie to go and train. I certainly never neglected any duties as a father, but it was hard to balance the amount of training I had to undergo with being a parent and husband.

The training schedule was brutal, but thorough. Just as I had enough of running, the plan called for swimming. It was certainly an excellent training program. I trained though the winter, counting the days until the big payoff. I also counted the fundraising that just kept coming. From the start, we were always ahead of the projections needed to hit the goal. It felt like the entire community was backing me in my efforts, which only pushed me to train harder and represent as well as I could.

April of 2010 brought along a unique opportunity. Brook, Elliana and I were on vacation for a week in Newport, Rhode Island enjoying the rest and relaxation. Near the end of our stay, I got a phone call from a representative at a medical company called Medtronic. I was told that I had been selected as a Medtronic Global Hero. Medtronic, I learned, was a valve very similar to the Medtronic. The representative explained that every year, the company hosts a ten mile road race. However, all of the runners of this race must meet several requirements. First, they have to be nominated; one can't simply sign up for the race. In addition, the runners must benefit from medical technologies somehow. Through this process, Medtronic selects twenty-five individuals from around the world to participate in this race.

I was honored to be nominated and selected for this amazing event. The mechanical valve that kept my heart pumping allowed me to still be able to do martial arts and all of my training for Ironman certainly was invaluable. I agreed to attend the race and thanked the representative. I thought that would be the end of the call, but the rep went on to inform me that Medtronic would be paying for my travel expenses both ways, as well as for Brook and Elliana. Not only that, but we were being put up in a luxurious hotel and given cash to spend in the city upon arrival. I laughed in amazement and thanked the representative several times. I hung up the phone and told my wife everything I had just heard. The race was going to be held in October in Minneapolis, after the Ironman race.

This was an awesome opportunity, and I was looking forward to having the privilege to experience it.

The next two months were filled with intense training as well as races here and there to be as prepared for Ironman as possible. I did several sprint distance triathlons (which I finished, I might add) as well as a half-Ironman race, a 70.3 mile prelude to the real deal. Even though this event is not necessary to compete in the full-length Ironman, it was an excellent indication of how the full race would be. The race was so close. I wanted it more than anything. Every time I went out for training or a smaller race, it was on my mind. I thought about it before bed and when I woke up. I would occasionally daydream about it at the gym while working. It was everywhere. Either in the form of fundraising, training or a news story in a local paper, the race enveloped me.

Just weeks before the race, one of my clients from work mentioned that he had just bought a duplex and was looking to get some new tenants. I went home that night and discussed it with Brook. It sounded like what we had been looking for. The next day at work, I talked with him and told him we would like to be those tenants. And sure enough, in the early days of July, we moved in to our new place.

It was a beautiful place. The kitchen and dining room were located immediately inside. A hallway led to the living room on the left, along with a bedroom downstairs. Beside the living room, stairs led up to several more rooms upstairs, including a spacious attic with a side room that I saw a lot of potential in for an office (i.e. a mancave).

Even a week after moving in, there were still so many unpacked boxes. With Brook's busy schedule and my last week of peak training in full swing, there was almost no time to furnish our new place. The bright side was that Ellie loved playing with all of the boxes lying around.

Just a week before our trip to New York for the Ironman race, the Nature Conservancy held a final fundraiser at a local theatre in

Concord. All of our campaign's major supporters were in attendance. The entire theatre was packed, even with standing room provided. The event featured a video of my training, along with several testimonials that allowed the supporters to see what was involved in training for Ironman. I, along with several other individuals including the Governor and his wife, spoke to the crowd. We thanked them for all of their support and donations.

Then Daryl got up and spoke. "Good evening everyone and thank you all for coming out. Tonight, I have an exciting announcement to make." I wondered what on earth it could be. With only a week left for fundraising, we were barely over the halfway mark for our goal. "There is a member of the Conservancy here tonight that has made an unbelievable offer. If we are able to raise ten thousand dollars during this event tonight, he will write a check for *one hundred thousand dollars* on the spot."

A buzz immediately filled the room. I thought I had heard Daryl wrong. I turned to Brook and asked her what he had just said. She confirmed that I had, in fact, heard him correctly. If we could raise ten thousand dollars tonight, this individual's donation would propel us past our fundraising goal. The event went on as planned, with several other videos playing while the guests were allowed to mingle and help themselves to appetizers and beverages.

For the rest of the event, people were going crazy over the announcement Daryl had made. From what I heard from the main fundraising staff in attendance, people were donating left and right: from one-hundred dollars to five-hundred dollars and everything in between. Within just a half hour, 14,000 dollars had been raised, and just as it had been announced, the gentleman wrote out a check for one hundred thousand dollars for the Nature Conservancy. This incredibly generous donation careened us up to $190,000 in total fundraising. The board of trustees and I exchanged high fives and congratulations and hugs. It was a special moment for everyone involved. Daryl commented that he had never seen anything like the degree of support shown tonight from the community. I felt giddy with excitement. One moment I had been disappointed that we would fall completely short of our goal, and the next minute the fundraising goal was left in the dust. I will be forever grateful to all of the individuals that supported me in my efforts to raise funds for a great cause. Surpassing my goal for fundraising put me in an excellent mood for the trip out to New York.

The time to leave for Lake Placid came sooner than expected. We had been contacted several weeks prior by a woman who played a huge role with the Nature Conservancy in New York. She had heard of my fundraising efforts and had offered us use of a cottage on a property she owned while we were in town for the race. It was only about a half hour from Lake Placid. We thanked her and quickly accepted the offer. Once a half hour away from the cottage, we called the woman to announce our arrival. She confirmed the address and said she'd see us soon.

The cottage was on an estate that was shadowed by the Adirondacks. When we got there, we initially overlooked the cottage because of how large it was, assuming it was a mansion and the cottage was somewhere else on the property behind the mansion. This wasn't a small, beachside-style cottage. It was just gorgeous. The home on the property must have been worth somewhere in seven figures. There was a boathouse next to the cottage, with several boats resting inside. A deep blue lake sat at the foot of the mountain range, making for quite a beautiful sight.

Upon entering the cottage, we saw that it was just as decked out inside as it looked from the outside. The entire interior was wood, resembling a fancy log cabin. Cathedral ceilings vaulted upward in the main living area. A stone fireplace sat at the base of the living room, welcoming us in. The kitchen was large and open, with plenty of cute bits of décor scattered throughout. A loft towered over both of these areas, bright lights illuminating the upper area of the cottage. Overall, the cottage was bigger than our entire duplex. There was no detail not thought of. The furnishings in the cottage were all perfectly placed. And the views of the mountains and the lake that it overlooked couldn't be beat. Brook and I kept pointing out things to one another; a nice piece of furniture here, an amazing view of the lake and mountains there.

The woman who was kind enough to offer us use of her cottage was there when we arrived. She welcomed us in and gave us a quick tour of the cottage, explaining that we had free reign of the place while we were there. Over dinner the first night, she introduced us to her husband, a successful investor in New York. The two were probably in their late fifties, and full of energy. We got to know each other over dinner that night. The wife was very curious about my training and lead-up to Ironman, and I was more than willing to provide a summary of my training. I was humbled as I gained a bird's eye view over my progress as I relayed it to our hosts. I had come a long way, and the magnitude of what I was about to attempt started to set in.

The next few days consisted of easy training and lots of eating. I ate so much that I felt like a bear preparing for hibernation. During my training, I enjoyed taking in the beauty the region had to offer. I found myself focusing more on the scenery displayed around me than the training itself. After some last minute training, Brook and I sat down for dinner (Ellie was already asleep) in the cottage to enjoy our last meal together before the race. We decided to eat out on the back porch, which had the beautiful backdrop of the Adirondacks. The blood-red sunlight pouring over the tips of the mountain range and trickling down into the lake made for quite a view. We tried to make small talk, but we both felt the weight of tomorrow pressing down on us. "So do you think you're ready?" Brook asked me as she leaned back in her chair. I thought about the question. I wasn't sure how to answer, thinking about the question over a mouthful of food.

"I don't think I'd ever be one hundred percent ready for something as big as this, no matter what I did. But I think that the training I've done has me as prepared as I can be," I answered. With a race like Ironman, there are no guarantees or measures that are foolproof. There's only 'as prepared as possible', 'as ready as can be'. And that's where I was.

We had agreed to stay the last night before the race at my parents' hotel which was only two miles from the start of the race, rather than the fifteen miles away of the cottage. They asked the same question that Brook had over dinner, and I replied with the same answer I had given before. For most of the night, my parents played with their granddaughter and we all caught up with each other. Brook and I told my parents about our new place while they shared stories about when they moved into their first house together, offering pointers and tips to us the whole time.

That night was a restless one for me. I was full of nerves and anxious about what was ahead of me. I slept a little bit here and there, but kept tossing and turning and waking up every half hour. I finally gave up at three A.M as the cloak of darkness started lifting. Even though I had next to no sleep, I felt rested and physically ready for the day. I had several slices of peanut butter toast coupled with a banana for breakfast and chased them with glasses of juice and water. I looked out the hotel at the horizon. Sunrise was still several hours off, but faint light was starting to peek through the clouds. It was very calming to just look out at the skyline.

At four a.m., I hopped in the shower and then threw on my race clothes. I chuckled at the memory from four short years ago when I was wearing baggy basketball shorts and cheap goggles at the start of my first triathlon. Now, I would use those sprint distance triathlons as warm-ups for Ironman. I had come quite a long way since then. I was now a father. I had undergone open-heart surgery after heart failure. I was an established and successful fitness trainer in Concord. And today I was going to give everything I had in the hopes that I could add the title of Ironman to my resume.

There would be a shuttle passing through the town that would pick up the racers and bring us to the start of the swim. However, I opted to walk the distance to the start. It was just less than two miles, so it wasn't anything crazy. I wrote a note for my family and left it on the kitchen counter letting them know where I was. This walk also gave me time to clear my mind and focus on the task ahead. I tried to envision how the day might go. I knew there was no certainty in anything, but I had done my homework. I was prepared. I was ready. In addition to my extensive training, I had an amazing coach that had made sure I was as prepared as possible.

My bike had been racked the night before as per race rules. All of my bags with food and drinks had been packed away and given to volunteers the day before. One year ago, I had been in their shoes. Now I was a competitor. Experiencing firsthand the work these volunteers do made me appreciate it that much more. For each leg of an Ironman, there must be several hundred volunteers. It really is incredible.

I made my way to the swim-to-bike transition point. I pumped some extra air in the tires for good measure. I then made my way to the start to get my body marked and get my bib (the marker with my race number attached to my race clothes). I got my race number marked on my shoulder and hand. I also got my age on that race day marked on my right calf: 32 years young. I was racer 111 that day.

The race had over 2,700 participants. Many of them were first-time racers like me. It was a rather cool morning, so everyone was moving around to keep warm. I knew that many of these first-timers were about to have goals and dreams come true today, just as I would. It filled me with awe to look around at the amount of fellow competitors. Each person standing around me had trained as hard as I did, each person had a story that was about to unfold. I scanned the crowd and saw Brook and Ellie standing in the front. Brook waved me over. I walked up to my girls and got one last kiss from both of them for good luck. I turned back and took a few deep breaths. It was game time.

I slipped on my wetsuit over my race clothes and then put my swim cap on. I got into the water about ten minutes before the start of the race. The pros had just gone out, since they started before the rest of the field. I looked over my left shoulder and saw Daryl in the crowd. He was holding a gigantic camera in his hand. He waved to me and I waved back. For some reason, this small action calmed my nerves.

I then did something I had first seen four years ago: I walked a little bit farther out from shore and added my own personal touch to Lake Placid. After relieving myself of some water weight, I walked to the start of the swim just as the announcer called for everyone to do the same. We all flocked to the start. We must have looked like a group of skinny penguins, all wearing similar wetsuits and white swim caps, flapping our arms around and shaking our bodies every now and then. I wasn't a fast swimmer, so I decided to start near the back of the group to minimalize the potential for any injury. I looked out onto the lake and saw a line of kayaks and buoys lining the main race loop for us to follow.

The full weight of the race hit me as I stood there and looked out onto the lake, waiting for the gun to signal the start of the race. I had trained tirelessly to get here. I had put myself through so much to prepare for this moment. I was about to take the first leap in the most physically demanding race the world has to offer. My muscles were tensed, ready to spring into action. I closed my eyes and tried to slow my heartbeat. I could feel my chest resonating with each pump, each tick of my heart. I was ready.

Tedy Bruschi, my daughter Elliana and me

Jumping to avoid a sword in early 2000's

My karate instructor Jeff Hardy and me

Post Ironman with Brook and Elliana

My wife Brook and me

Running into the finisher's chute at Ironman

High-fiving my dad at Ironman

With my brother Jamie after we finished the 2016 Boston Marathon together

My daughter Isla and me

My daughter Bryn and me

Part Four – The Race of my Life

Chapter Twelve
The Swim

Bang! The gunshot lanced through the air like a whip. The front line of competitors dove into the water as if they had springs in their legs. I watched from the back of the pack. It was complete chaos in the water. It looked like a giant blender. I couldn't even make out which arms and legs belonged to which body. People were crashing into one another, getting smacked and kicked constantly and trying to get enough space to maneuver. I decided to hang back for about thirty seconds to allow the action to die down. Looking around, I saw that there were many people that shared the same thought. Once the coast was relatively clear, I entered the water with the back of the group and started the race.

The first five minutes of the swim felt like being in a washing machine. One second I was fine, the next I was turned to the side because of another racer being close to me and the moment after that I was on my back. I couldn't get into a rhythm. I had to devote more energy to being aware of my surroundings than the actual swim. I kept trying to glance outward to make sure I was staying within the track and not veering off course. The sound of thousands of arms and legs pushing through the water was thunderous. It was alarming, but since my first triathlon I had worked on staying calm in these conditions. Right from the first few minutes of the swim I noticed I was taking in a lot of water but didn't let it affect me too much.

The swim was two loops straight out and straight back to the beach. Once we got just over half a mile out from the shore, there was a sharp bank to the left and a straight shot back to the beach. People were passing me in the swim, but I wasn't worried about it. I had trained properly and knew my pace was good enough that I didn't have to worry about it. I just had to make sure that no accidents or unforeseen circumstances interfered with my pace. As I made the turn, I was spitting out water with nearly every stroke. I could hear the rhythmic clap of a helicopter hovering above the lake and knew that there was a camera crew taking pictures of the race below; I had seen them snapping photos when I had volunteered in years past.

I finished the first lap and got out of the water for the short run across the beach. I took the time as I jogged back to where I had started to think about how I felt physically. I was feeling good. My breathing was heavy, but I was alright. I had been careful not to push myself in the first lap and didn't let the commotion of the close quarters get to me.

I immediately noticed that the second lap was easier than the first due to a lack of congestion. As I was starting my second lap, some of the pros were already getting out of the water from their second lap and transitioning into the bike portion of the race. I was finally able to find my rhythm in the swim. As my arms cut through the cool New York water, I flashed back to a moment I had experienced several years ago.

When I visited Lake Placid to watch the race in 2008, I had jumped in the water with my friend Rich on the day before the race. We started to swim and headed toward the line of buoys with the kayaks that marked the boundaries for the swim. Rich challenged me to swim to the first buoy, several hundred yards from shore. I was able to make it, but I was winded. I grasped at the buoy for support, but it provided none.

I thought that we were done and I started back to shore. Instead, Rich challenged me to try to get to the next buoy out. I grimaced and started swimming toward it. It was terrifying to be out in the middle of the massive lake. After taking a quick break and looking around at my wide open surroundings, I panicked. "Dude, forget this, I'm turning around and heading back!"

"Uh, no way man, we're going to keep going. Let's go," he said as he headed farther out from the safety of shore. As much as I was freaking out, the thought of swimming back alone freaked me out more. I cursed Rich in my head as I followed him farther out of my comfort zone.

When we were swimming, I was able to see a line of rope just under the surface that connected the buoys to one another. I was able to keep my head down and follow this from buoy to buoy. I wanted to quit with every stroke. But every time I was about to stop and tread water, Rich egged me on to keep going. Eventually I finished the circuit by collapsing on the beach and not moving for a long time, gasping air like a fish out of water.

This memory played through my head as I passed by a buoy on my second lap. Two years ago I could barely complete one circuit, and now I was cruising through my second lap. 'I'm in a good place now,' I thought. I focused on just getting to the buoy in front of me, then the next. Fragmenting the circuit made it much easier to process mentally. I was also generally following one competitor in front of me that was holding almost the exact same pace as I was. At the turnaround for the second lap I peeked at my watch. I was making good time. The rest of the swim was fairly uneventful and I walked up the shore with plenty of time before the cut off.

I jogged toward the transition area and approached a group of volunteers that were known as 'wetsuit strippers'. Essentially, these volunteers were a human version of a racing pit stop. I just stood there as they worked to remove my wetsuit. As the crew worked, I recognized one of the volunteers: my friend Ryan! I had trained with Ryan many times and had the utmost respect for him. He lit up with a bright smile and asked how I was doing. "Great, ready for the rest of the race!" Ryan got the suit off and he wished me good luck on the rest of my race. I thanked him and started the short run to the transition.

As I ran I was slightly disoriented from the time that I had spent being horizontal in the water. My legs felt slightly wobbly for a few minutes. After a few hundred yards, I had adjusted to being back on land. Once I was at the bike rack I grabbed my bike and took some cleansing breaths to relax. I had made it through the swim. Now I was about to start the longest portion of the race, the bike ride.

Chapter Thirteen
The Ride

Before heading out onto the course, I biked over to the spectator area and saw my family. I gave Brook and Ellie high fives and kisses, then exchanged high fives with my Mom and Dad. I turned away from the crowd with a grin on my face. The quick interaction with my family provided a jolt of motivation and energy.

As I pedaled onto the start of the course, I noticed that the ground looked wet, as if a light rain had passed through the area. I thought it was odd that I hadn't noticed it while swimming. I quickly put it out of my mind and shifted my focus to the bike ride ahead of me. The start was fairly flat, and like the swim, was also a looped course. However, unlike the swim, the bike ride was a two loop ride. Twenty eight miles into town and twenty eight miles back performed twice.

Right from the start, the surroundings were breathtaking. Not that the scenery wasn't great on the lake, but I hadn't exactly been able to stop and sightsee in the middle of the lake while thousands of other bodies were in the water around me. I looked around at the mountains off in the distance that made up the Adirondack range. Different shades of green dotted the hills. A dense tree cover lined both sides of the road. Every now and then, one side of the road gave way to a view of a massive mountainside shrouded in foliage, about to put on a color display with the change of seasons.

The course itself was very hilly. The first couple of miles were a slight climb, and my legs took some time to get used to the grade. I was feeling off from all of the water I had taken in during the swim. In retrospect, this made me go a lot slower in the first section of the ride than I could have. I peeked at the GPS on my watch early on and saw that I was five miles in. 'Oh boy, five down, one hundred and seven to go,' I joked to myself. I ran numbers in my head and figured that the remainder of the distance was equivalent to biking from my house to Boston, and then back again.

I had already passed a few people in the race as I reached an awesome descent from the hilly introduction to the course. The descent offered some truly amazing views of the Adirondack range. The mountains towered over me and seemed to look down upon me as I made my way down the hill. The wind whipped over my helmet, producing a soft whistling noise. There wasn't a cloud in the sky and the sun was relentless, a stark contrast to the downpour of last year.

Even though I was making up a decent amount of time, I wasn't about to try to beat anyone; I just wanted to enjoy the journey I was on and the scenery surrounding me. But I couldn't spend my time sightseeing, I had to focus on the task at hand. Thirty miles into the ride, my mind starting playing games with itself. I remember asking myself what I was doing and why. I had already spent an hour and forty minutes in the water and almost the same amount of time on the bike. I starting second guessing my preparation I had done for the race. 'Should I have eaten more? My stomach is upset, is that from hunger or the water intake from the swim?' This thought process started to stress me out. At this point, the devil on my shoulder said that I could just hop off the bike at the next aid station and volunteer as I had the year before.

I did my best to shake off these thoughts. They nagged at me here and there, but tucking my head and gutting it out helped to hold them at bay. Whenever the thoughts came back, I forced myself to take every sensory detail in around me - a feel of the wind crawling over my arms, a constant *whizz* of my wheels, a clean scent of the mountain air, a soft rush of the air parting over my helmet, a faint aftertaste of banana and sports drink. The more I focused on the moment and task at hand, the less nagging thoughts I had.

The fiftieth mile came up quickly. I was almost at the turnaround, only six more miles before I got to see my family again. The last six miles were more of a climb than the main body of the loop. My legs were shot by the middle of the climb into town. But I buckled down and made it through the climb to the sight of a huge cheering crowd. The body of spectators was so large that I could hear them before I actually saw them. My surroundings started changing from wide open areas to city streets. Mountains gave way to civilization and the quiet ride was suddenly filled with a buzz of energy.

As I neared the turnaround, I saw my family in the crowd. As per my normal routine, I went up and gave hugs and kisses and got the same in return. Some of the spectators were starting to walk from the turnaround area to other areas within the course. Brook asked how I was doing. Through labored breaths, I replied, “It’s all good, it’s a beautiful course. Do you have any sunscreen I can grab?” She handed me a bottle and I lathered it on my arms and face. I could already feel a light burn developing and didn’t want to look like a lobster when I crossed the finish line.

I waved goodbye to my girls and headed back out onto the course for the second half of the ride. Unfortunately, the climb into town did not translate to a descent out of town. I was immediately bummed out. ‘Seriously? I have to do this again? What gives?!’ I thought. It was hard to get back into a rhythm and I had to really push to get through the initial climb. Right from the start of the ride back, my mind started with the games, this time worse than before. But every time my mind threw out the possibility to just quit and call it a day, I refused and pushed through. I knew I had to finish this race. I had put too much time and effort into preparing for this to quit now. Quitting was not an option at all. The only choice I had was how hard I would ride.

During the entire bike ride I found myself falling back into an age -old habit: I ran my martial arts forms in my head. Not only did this help the time pass, but it also took my mind off the condition of my body; the burning in my quads or the fatigue all over. There was something calming about practicing mental martial arts on the course. It cleared up everything on my mind and allowed me to refocus on the race.

Miles seventy through eighty brought me back to the relatively flat area of the course. In this time, I saw many of my friends that passed me on their way into town. The bike loop was on one road, so I passed them as they were making their way into town. We waved and yelled greetings at one another. This was the first point that I actually felt good on the bike ride. I had a solid rhythm going and I was dialed in to the task at hand. I dug into a protein goo formula and more of my sports drink during this time. Even my stomach was feeling better! A fellow competitor rode up next to me and started talking to me. At first I thought it was odd, but then welcomed the interaction. We talked for ten or fifteen miles, then he took off into the distance.

I was nearing the one hundred mile mark when I realized that I had only gone to the bathroom once since that start of the race. I thought that I should have gone more than that and maybe I should take in more liquids to compensate. I drained the rest of my sports drink for good measure.

Finally, I broke past the one hundred mile marker. I was really feeling it at this point, my legs were totally shot. What didn't help was seeing other racers walking for short durations, a tempting thought but one that I knew would backfire for me, as I'd get too comfortable and want to walk longer than I should. I started to realize that I may have pushed it too hard for the past twenty to twenty-five miles because of the flat grade. I knew that I now had to go through a steady climb up a hill for the next eight or nine miles, the same hill that had been an excellent descent in the beginning of the ride. I knew this last climb was essentially the end of the loop. After this hill it was a slight descent to the transition area for the marathon. All that stood between me and the end of the ride was this one hill.

My watch indicated that I was on mile 105 out of 112. I was right there, only another seven miles and I was done. Also, the last two miles were a downhill cruise from this side of the loop. Suddenly, both of my quads seized up. Startled, I pulled over to the side of the course. I winced in pain as I placed a foot on the ground. I reached for a banana from my food bag. I knew I needed fuel badly. I wolfed it down. I massaged the muscle as I wondered if I could finish the race. I was genuinely unsure if I could do this. "Come on man, you're right there. Four more miles and then a coast to the transition. *COME ON,*" I said out loud to myself. It took three minutes of massaging my legs before biting the bullet and hopping back on the bike.

I pushed myself harder than ever before on a bike, and after having my legs seize two more times, I finally made it to the top of the hill. I was able to look down over the last two miles of road to the transition. Little dots that were competitors moved over the road near the end of the course in front of me. I could see the large band that was the group of spectators waiting at the transition. Like in town, I could hear them before I had even reached the top of the hill, a faint roar in the distance. Now that I was getting closer to the finish of the bike ride, the roar increased and the energy level rose. That energy alone was what carried me to the end of the bike course. I coasted into the finish area and hopped off my bike.

As I jogged to the transition area I looked into the crowd, where, of course, I found Brook and the rest of my family near the front. This instantly lifted my spirits. Despite my burning legs and upset stomach, I smiled and felt uplifted. I waved to them and handed my bike to a volunteer waiting to take it and store it away. She looked in my eyes as I handed the bike to her. "So how was the ride? Nice views?"

"Nice views. But honestly, I never want to see that damn wheeled terror ever again," I threw out bluntly. She laughed at my remark.

"Yeah, that's not the first time I've heard that today, that's for sure. Well you're almost there, go get 'em!" she encouraged. I smiled and started walking over to my family. I checked my watch to see that I had made the bike cut off by well over an hour. I had plenty of time to spare. I felt the most comfortable with the marathon out of all of the legs of the race, so I figured I had this in the bag.

Before heading out for the run, I wanted to get my legs checked out. I went to the medical tent where there were several Active Release Therapy (A.R.T) workers stationed. I approached a vacant area and explained my issue and what I was feeling. The worker nodded and asked me to sit in a booth next to him. He worked for three or four minutes on each leg, and like flipping a switch, I felt so much better after that. I thanked him multiple times. He laughed me off and, like the bike volunteer, told me to finish in style.

I ran out onto the transition area and starting making my way toward my family near the start of the marathon. As I did, I heard someone calling from behind me. I turned around to see a volunteer running at me with something in her hand. I stopped and let her catch up. As she got to me, she shouted, "Do you want some sunscreen?!" I nodded and held out my hands, but was surprised when my hands were covered in it. She didn't just give me a normal amount of sunscreen; she gave me so much that it was dripping through my fingers. I laughed and thanked her as I ran to the crowd, trying to do damage control with the sunscreen the entire way.

I ran up to the Jeremy cheerleading crew in the crowd and instantly gave my wife and daughter a huge kiss. I embraced both of my parents at the same time. I pulled away and gave my dad a high five. I learned later that a photographer took a shot of my father and I high-fiving each other at that moment. We're both beaming with ear-to-ear grins, and it is a snapshot that I cherish to this day.

After hearing 'good luck babe' and 'you got this Jeremy' I turned and stared down the road in front of me. I had completed the two-lap swim. I had grinded through the insane amount of bike riding. Two of the three legs of the race were done. I had one leg of the race left. I had time to spare as well. This was it, the marathon. The end of Ironman. I fueled up with food and drink, reassured myself and started down the road to the finish line.

Chapter Fourteen
The Run

The weather report had said that clouds would move in between four and six in the evening. It looked like the clouds were going to hold off until the latter end of that time frame, as the sun was beating down on me as I started the run. At least with the bike and swim I had relief in either the water or the wind. Here I had nothing. Even with a visor on, I still felt the sun radiating on my face. Sunglasses did a little bit to help with the glare, but I was still squinting as I ran.

I had started running a bit before five thirty. I had dismounted the bike just before five, but the visit to the ART worker and seeing my family had tacked on some time before the start of the marathon. Right from the beginning of the run, my legs felt heavy, as though I had just done a bunch of heavy squats. It seemed like I had a ten pound weight attached to each ankle. This is where my training really paid off; I had prepared for this scenario through 'brick runs', which consist of going from a long bike ride to running with a quick transition. This mimics the heavy-footed feeling I was feeling, hence the name.

However, no matter how much one trains, an Ironman is an Ironman. I got to the first mile and groaned. 'Seriously, 25 more of those?!' I thought. I forced my complaints down and kept on trudging. The marathon was the same format as the bike; one loop out away from town, then a turnaround and a run back into town and across the finish line.

The first 5k distance, roughly three-and-a-half miles, was routine. The next 5k, however, was mentally brutal. That persistent devil on my shoulder reappeared. I remember thinking bluntly, 'This bites. Just bites.' But then I made an effort to look at what I had going for me. I had raced 120 miles to that point. I only had a fraction of the race left. I looked up from my feet and noticed that the sun was starting to dip lower over the Adirondacks. This reminded me of the sunlight spilling over the peaks that I had seen a few nights ago from the cottage with Brook.

All I had was time at this point in the race, and I was alone with my thoughts which shifted to the journey that had brought me to this point. I started reliving everything that got me to that road that night. Brook. Ellie. My parents. My thoughts shifted to my support team. I thought about all of the backing I had from everyone in my life. Giving any less than one hundred percent would be a disservice to them, and to myself. I had practically been on my death bed when I had made the promise that I would finish an Ironman. I had worked too hard to get here, to get this far in the race, only to back out. No, this was my time to shine.

But man, I was beat. Just as I had during the bike ride, I thought about the martial arts tests I had undergone to earn my ranks of black belt. This topic blocked out everything else for three miles. I thought about what I had gone through to get to where I was in martial arts. At times during the testing process, I had been keeled over in a corner of the hay field that we tested in, wondering how I was going to make it through the rest of the day. But just putting one more go in on a technique or one more run through of a form got me closer to the end of the test. That was exactly what I was doing here. Each mile I ran was one more mile in the books, and one mile closer to the finish.

As much as I pushed myself, there was only so long I could keep up the constant run. Halfway through the marathon I was forced to walk for thirty seconds. My body was running low on fuel and I was sick of the sports drinks from the aid stations. The sun had set over the horizon, giving way to a dark crimson skyline as the moon rose overhead. This also brought cooler air on the course, which was a relief. However, I was still drenched with sweat. At the aid stations scattered across the course, they offered sponges soaked in cold water. Squeezing these over my head felt great for about ten seconds, but then the effect wore off and gave way to the semi-cool temperatures on the course.

The aid stations started to have less value for me as I ran farther and farther. The stations offered cookies, bananas, oranges, grapes and even pretzels for the run. As much as I was running on an empty stomach, I had to be careful not to give in to temptation and fill myself up. As for beverages, the choices consisted of the usual water and sports drinks, with the occasional flat cola being held out to the racers.

Just past some of the aid tents was a special needs station in which racers had personalized food and beverages stored the night before. A volunteer at the aid stations would announce my race number and name via megaphone. At the special needs station, a meticulously organized staff would grab the bag I provided them the night before and offer me the contents. The whole operation was run very systematically. As I mentioned before, I cannot stress enough the amazing work the volunteers do at Ironman. In the special needs bag I had packed a small brownie and a pb&j sandwich, a far and welcome cry from the aid station's food.

As I finished my brownie in several bites, a fellow racer ran up next to me. The first thing I noticed about this individual was his physique; the best way to describe it was 'completely ripped'. The guy was in amazing shape. We immediately struck up conversation as evening turned to night. He reminded me of a past client of mine in every respect. His mannerisms, looks, build and everything all reminded me of a guy named Doug that I had coached in the past. I asked if that was who he was, to which he replied, "Not me, my name's Bill." I think he could tell that I was fading and a little grumpy, because he was very cheerful during our talks.

Side-by-side with Bill was an excellent way to run the rest of the race. When I ran, he ran. When I slowed to a walk temporarily, he stuck right next to me. We talked about anything and everything that came to mind. He told me a story about something his two daughters had done last week; I told him about Elliana. He told me where he was from and that he worked in DC for a big pharmaceutical company, and I told him about New Hampshire and my work as a personal fitness trainer. I learned that he had raced all over the world, but just like me, this was his first Ironman race. He was curious about why I was racing. "What made you decide to put in the effort to train for this and compete?" he asked.

I thought about how to answer. I wasn't sure if I wanted to tell him about my health history, as I was worried the subject matter would dampen my spirits talking about all of those hardships. At first I didn't, I simply told him that three years ago I had made myself a promise to finish an Ironman race, and that I felt the progression from shorter triathlons to Ironman was a natural one. It didn't take long before I filled him in on the rest of the story. A couple miles into my run with Bill, I brought up my history of endocarditis and heart failure, and how I had made that promise while in the hospital. I explained what I had gone through before being admitted at the hospital and what it had taken to get here. After I was done, he was silent. I glanced at him, and moonlight illuminated his face to show his shocked expression.

"Seriously?! That is an AMAZING story you have! Man, I'm over here complaining about sore muscles leading up to the race and you've gone through all of that? And now you're here, running to the finish line of Ironman?! Jeremy, you're an absolute animal, I don't even know what to say." It felt great to hear all of this from a traveled racer as in shape as Bill.

Throughout the last half of the marathon, Bill and picked each other up when the other was in a funk. When I was fading, he would reel me back into the run, and when he was feeling it I reined him back into the moment. We fed off each other's energy and performance. Through this and our talks we developed a friendship, the kind of friendship that normally takes years to forge. In a matter of hours we were like brothers that had been separated at birth.

Seeing each other persevere through the difficulty of the last leg of Ironman and helping one another along was what solidified this bond. I certainly would have made it through the last leg of the race regardless, as would Bill, but working with each other made it that much more manageable. He was that person that I really needed. To this day, I refer to Bill as 'my Ironman angel'.

The conversation then turned to the training we had done in preparation to get here. After describing all of the intense biking I had done, Bill threw out, "Today was the first time I had ever done more than one hundred miles on a bike in one day."

"What?!" I shouted out, taken aback. "Really? This was your first time with more than that in one day? Wow. How many triathlons had you participated in before this?"

"Three. This is my fourth triathlon," Bill said as if it was nothing. My eyes widened. I was shocked, but Bill was in such good shape that he could get away with it. I wished that I was able to pull that type of thing off. I had put thousands of hours of practice and triathlon experience in before attempting Ironman, and Bill was a rookie to triathlons altogether. Yet here he was, keeping me going through the marathon. His positive attitude was infectious. Every time we ran by a volunteer he made a point to thank them and give them a high five, a habit that I quickly adopted.

It was well into the night and very dark as we approached the end of the course. Because of this, volunteers had handed us glow sticks that we put on so that we were easily recognized and they could see us coming at the aid stations. We were almost completely burnt out at this point, and the running with bits of walking turned into walking with bits of running. We knew that we just needed to get close to the 24th mile before we saw the ski jumps. Two ski jumps sit side by side, looming over the road in Lake Placid. One jump is 90 meters long, and the other is 120 meters long. Both were built for and used in the 1980 Olympic Games. These jumps sit on a hill overlooking the road, so they can't be missed. Those two giants are indicators to runners that the end of the course has begun, and the finish line is just ahead.

Sure enough, the jumps came into view as we passed the 23rd mile mark. We knew that we would soon be taking a sharp right for a slight climb back into the downtown area of Lake Placid. The announcer's voice was booming through the valley as we approached the finish line somewhere in the vicinity of the speakers and noise. The fact that we could hear the sounds of the finish line from several miles away shows how big of an event Ironman really is.

There wasn't a cloud in the sky. The many stars sparkled overhead against a black skyline. The moon was beaming down, illuminating the road in front of us. Even though I had changed my shirt underneath my racing suit, I was dealing with a cold sweat. We got into town with two miles to go in the race. We were almost done. The way the end of the course is set up, we ran in and saw the domed finish line less than a hundred feet away from us. However, we had to turn onto a strip of road perpendicular to us, run a mile down and a mile back.

My senses were all on overdrive at this point. I was overwhelmed by the sight of such a large crowd. I heard the roar of the spectators mixed with the music and the announcer over the speakers. Even though

I was walking, the pavement felt like it was pounding up into my feet. The closest runner to Bill and I was a couple hundred feet in front of us, and we couldn't see anyone behind us. A clock on a pole in the crowd showed us we had over an hour left, so we had plenty of time. Racers that had already finished were either cheering on other racers, hanging out in the crowd or walking back up the road and to their cars. Bill and I were shoulder to shoulder as we neared the final loop.

Just as Bill and I turned onto the last strip of road for the final two miles, my favorite song came on over the speakers; I hadn't been on the strip for ten seconds when I heard, "*Everybody was Kung Fu Fighting!*" blare out over the crowd. I laughed and shook my head. 'Brook must have asked them to play this!' I thought, thinking there was no way this was a coincidence. 'Well, this is it. This is the end of the race, this is my time,' I thought to myself, feeling a wave of immense anticipation wash over me.

Bill and I fast walked up the strip for the first of the last two miles. As we neared the point to turn around and run the last mile, we both felt the anticipation building. He turned to me and said something that filled me with emotion. "Jeremy, this is your night. We have one mile to go. Once we turn around, *we are not stopping* until we cross that finish line. Lead the way, my friend." I was choked up. Tears welled up and threatened to overflow onto my cheeks. A warm lump formed high in my throat and I nodded my head tersely in acknowledgement. I put my hand on Bill's shoulder and we exchanged a knowing look that I will never forget. I turned around and stared down the last mile of our race. This had turned from my Ironman to our Ironman. We were both going to run the last mile together, cross the finish line together, and become Ironmen together.

That last mile was so emotional. The crowd was packed so tightly, there was no space between anyone. We were high fiving everyone holding out their arms as we ran. The energy level was insane, I fed off of it as I saw the finish line getting closer. Every step I took, it loomed larger. It was only a few hundred yards away. Then one hundred yards. A hundred feet. I was seconds away. I pushed into a full sprint as I ran across the finish line. *"Jeremy Woodward, you are an Ironman,"* pulsated through the crowd. I had done it. Wow. I had done it. I had finished an Ironman. I was ecstatic. I jogged to a stop and embraced Bill as we laughed and cried at what we had just accomplished. I wished him good luck with everything in the future, thanked him and told him I would never forget all he had done for me that night. Once we parted ways, I made my way over to the crowd to start searching for my family.

I saw my wife and daughter right away. Ellie looked like she had just woken up. Brook's smile, like a beacon, lit up the entire crowd. I ran over and locked them in a tight embrace. I was dripping sweat but it didn't matter. I heard Brook congratulate me and say how proud she was of me. If she said anything else, it was lost to the sheer volume of the crowd coupled with my mind reeling from the feat I had just accomplished. There is no one way to describe my emotions in that moment. I couldn't stop smiling, I was ready to cry, all while laughing the whole time. I pulled away and gave both of them a kiss, then made my way to the food tent.

Now that I had started to wind down, my stomach was winding up and demanding food. I immediately had a piece of pizza. From the first bite, it tasted like fine dining at a fancy restaurant. As much as I wanted to inhale every piece of food in the tent, I let the slice of pizza settle for fear of getting a cramp from eating too much too quickly. I chased the pizza with a can of soda then went over to the volunteer tent and asked for my bike and two transition bags. The volunteer took my race number and name and disappeared into the back of the tent. A minute later he reemerged with my bike and one bag. "Wait a minute," I started, “where’s the second bag?”

“There was only one back there man, sorry,” the volunteer explained with a shrug of his shoulders. I asked if I could go back there and look, and he agreed. After searching around, nothing turned up. The second bag had a pair of sneakers and some dry clothes, but nothing that was a huge loss. I was kind of bummed out that they had been lost, but I was mentally fried from the race and brushed it off. I grabbed my bike and bag before turning and walking back to Brook.

“Alright, I’m ready to head out of here. Where did you park?”

“Oh, it’s just up the road, I got a good spot. Are you ready?” I looked around one last time at the crowd. Yes, I was ready. I had done what I came to do. I was an Ironman. This was one of those moments that define a person for their entire life, and I knew that in that moment. I drank in that feeling, knowing how pivotal it was. I looked back in the direction of the finish line, where a significant amount of the crowd still stood, buzzing and cheering. I smiled at Brook and said I was ready to go. Brook smiled, turned and led the way to the car as we made our way out of the venue.

Chapter Fifteen
The Aftermath

My friend Ryan was kind enough to carry my bike to the car. Brook was carrying a sleeping Ellie, who had just gone through the longest day of her young life. Brook had said that the car was just around the corner from the finish line, but it certainly didn't feel like it. The walk of five hundred feet may as well have been a mountain. I was walking like I was a hundred years old. Then came the time for us to step up over the curb to get out of the road. While the other two didn't think anything of it, I looked at it thinking that it would be really hard. I stared down the curb like it owed me money. In retrospect, Brook admitted that she tried not to laugh in this moment at how ridiculous I looked staring down a strip of pavement.

I managed to get my left leg over the curbing without too much trouble. I could already feel that hiking my right leg up over the curb was going to be a lot harder. Just as I braced myself for the effort, my right leg locked up and cramped like nothing else. I had never experienced a cramp that bad. I remembered back to the end of the bike course and how my legs had seized and realized this must be related to my earlier incident. Ryan rushed to help me over the curb and half-assisted, half-carried me to the car.

Sitting down was bittersweet. It felt great to know I had accomplished my goal of Ironman and I could finally stop moving, but it felt odd to be stationary after seventeen hours of constant motion. We got into the car just after eleven, but before I knew it, the clock showed it was almost midnight. "Honey, can we stop somewhere and get something to eat? I'm starving." She agreed and we started looking for a place that was open. We saw the golden arches lit up down the road and turned into the McDonald's parking lot. My stomach growled in anticipation, but groaned when the front lights shut off just as Brook parked.

"No, no way this is happening right now," I complained. Brook knew how hungry I was, so she floored the car around to the drive-up. Luckily they still took our order. Brook went first with her order, asking for a small fry. Then it was my turn. Without hesitation, I leaned forward and said, "Could I have a large coke, large fry, two cheeseburgers, a milkshake and a slice of apple pie, please?" There was a long pause on the other end, as well as an amused look from Brook. After a few seconds, they reviewed our order and asked us to pull up.

I ate like I hadn't been fed in a week. I was already almost done one cheeseburger by the time Brook got back on the road. "Heart condition? No, I think the more pressing issue is that you have an endless stomach condition," she said sarcastically. I answered by mumbling a retort through my first bite of the second cheeseburger. I was done everything within fifteen minutes. Before we got back to the cottage, we had stopped again, this time at a 24-hour gas station. I walked out with a large soda and a brownie. As I chowed down and ignored eye rolls from Brook, we headed back to the cottage to get some rest.

We pulled into the designated parking spot for the cottage and I struggled to get out of the car. The dashboard clock read 12:55 A.M. As usual, I stubbornly refused assistance from my wife. We were both exhausted at this point, and dragged ourselves into the cottage. Brook went to put Ellie to bed as I walked through the giant cottage to one of many bathrooms. I hadn't been in an actual bathroom all day and needed it badly. I was alarmed when I saw that my pee was brown. My thoughts immediately turned to my heart. Had I pushed myself too hard by doing Ironman? Was this a side effect of a heart issue? Then I realized that it must have something to do with the ridiculous amount of cola and sports drinks that had kept me going that day. My system was completely shot. I had gone from running the race of my life on almost no solid food to eating all of the food I could get my hands on. I took my regular heart measurements to ensure that everything was alright, and I was correct. All readings were within my normal range.

With that issue off my chest, I stripped down and hopped in the shower for a much-needed wash. I spoiled myself and just stood underneath the showerhead for longer than I ever have. I almost fell into a trance as the water cascaded over my body. I closed my eyes and stood still, turning every now and then under the constant rush of water.

I opened my eyes and looked down at the curved scar on my chest that served as a reminder of what I had been through to get here. That scar reminded me that while I swam, biked and ran many miles during Ironman, it wasn't so long ago that I was working just as hard to walk around the ICU. A tissue valve had deteriorated underneath that scar, and now a mechanical valve worked constantly to ensure my heart kept pumping me onward. That mechanical valve had made the Ironman race possible. I realized that I had been zoning out in the shower for quite some time. I turned the handle to the 'off' position and the water went from a constant flow, to a tiny drip, to nothing. I grabbed a towel, dried myself off and changed into my comfy clothes for bed.

Brook was already asleep when I walked in, and Ellie was snoozing right next to her. I looked at this scene in front of me and felt a swell of pride. I had a beautiful wife and an equally beautiful daughter. Brook was the most supportive person I had ever met, and I could never thank her enough for everything she did and put up with. I walked over to Ellie and ran my hand through her blonde hair. I bent over and kissed her forehead. She wriggled slightly in her sleep, smacking her lips before lying still once again. I quietly snuck into bed so as to not disturb either of them. I gently kissed Brook on the back of her head and curled up to go to sleep.

I couldn't sleep much that night. I had just put my body through the hardest experience of my life, and hadn't stopped for seventeen hours. '*You are an Ironman*'. Those words had been reverberating through my head since getting back to the cottage. It was still surreal that I had achieved the goal I had been working toward for three years. I rolled over and tried to clear my mind - to no avail. My mind was a slideshow of moments from the race; feelings, sights and moments from the day were cycling through my head.

I didn't want to toss and turn too much in bed for fear of waking Brook up. She had also had a long day and deserved a good sleep. Between moving from one area to another and being on her feet the entire day while tending to Ellie, she was exhausted. She had woken up at five in the morning on race day and hadn't gotten to bed until almost two this morning. I was beyond appreciative of all the support she had shown through not only the race, but everything leading up to the race. Finally, I managed to fall asleep.

Five o'clock rolled around and I woke up. Before I even opened my eyes, I remembered what I had done the previous day. 'Oh wow, I'm an Ironman!' I thought as I felt a goofy grin cross my face at the recollection of my achievement. All of a sudden I was wide awake, thinking about all of the moments from the race. I decided I may as well get up since Brook had set an alarm for seven. I stood up slowly and stretched for a long moment. My body was sore all over and exhausted from the race. I looked down at my girls. Both of them were still asleep, and I wasn't about to disturb them. I glanced out the window at the skyline and decided to go sit outside and watch the sun rise. Feeling every mile that I had completed the previous day, I hobbled my way out of the bedroom into the kitchen, grabbed a few things and made my way outside, careful to be as quiet as possible.

The hill that the cottage sat on led down to the boathouse. I found a way that I could climb from the hill to the roof of the boathouse and made myself comfortable. It was a chilly morning with a light breeze; I had come prepared with two blankets, warm shoes, a fleece jacket and a hat. I laid one blanket out on the roof and wrapped the other around myself. I had also grabbed a bottle of iced tea from the cottage to sip on while I took in the view.

The mountain range towering over me formed a 'V' shape between two peaks. The skyline between the two peaks was a lighter hue than the other areas of the sky, making for a beautiful view. The peaks themselves had patches of rocky ledges that were surrounded by tightly packed trees. Shadows fell from trees that were on top of hills here and there on the mountainside. Tall pine trees poked through the canopy every now and then, as if they were on their tip-toes and peeking over the tops of other trees. The mass of trees gave way to two small meadows on the opposite bank from where I was. I thought I saw a deer darting into the woods next to one of the meadows. Large downed trees protruded from the shore out into the lake. The water was completely still that morning. A mirror reflection of the shore and trees formed in the water all across the lake; I could even see the reflection of one of the rocky outcroppings on the mountain. A light fog that had cloaked the lake was now in patchy clumps across the surface. In some places, it was so low to the water that it looked to be part of the lake itself.

The whole scene was perfect. I had two hours before my wife's alarm would ring, which left me plenty of time to calmly reflect on what

I had just done and to allow my mind to wander. I felt so many different emotions that morning. I felt overjoyed that I was an Ironman. I felt sad that the whole event had come to an end, but felt hopeful about what was to come. Curiosity at what the future might hold for me followed a feeling of anticipation at heading home. I reflected on all of this and knew that every one of these emotions had played some part in getting me to where I was today.

The horizon started to glow orange and then red, signaling the fast-approaching sunrise. Bands of sunlight started to break the foggy cover of clouds. I could see the sun starting to creep over the summits and knew that it must be close to seven. I grabbed my blankets and walked back up to the cottage, feeling refreshed.

After packing our things up, we had a quick breakfast and left a sincere thank you note on the kitchen table. Brook and I packed the car together. With one final look over my shoulder at the cottage and lake, we turned onto the road and started the trip back home.

The ride home from Lake Placid felt similar to the ride home from Tufts. Even though these two events were under completely opposite conditions, I knew on both occasions that I was heading home for a new chapter in my life. And just like after my valve replacement, I was excited to dive in and see what the future held for us.

Part Five—Finding my Own Rhythm in Life

Chapter Sixteen
Raising Awareness And Spirits

The week following Ironman was filled with congratulations from everyone I came across. Clients, family and friends all made it a point to go out of their way to congratulate me on my accomplishment. Even random members of the community came up to me on the street to comment on what I had done, both at Ironman and with fundraising for the Nature Conservancy. It felt great to know that all of these people were so supportive.

The Tuesday after finishing Ironman, I was in downtown Concord on Main Street. I had just picked up lunch. I was driving home when I got a call on my phone. I expected it to be Brook saying she wanted me to pick up something else on my way home. Instead, it was an unfamiliar number. I almost didn't answer it, guessing it was an accidental misdial. But I did pick it up and answered. I was greeted by a cheerful voice. "Hello Jeremy, my name is David Watkins. I have been following you for a while, and noticed your work for the Nature Conservancy with your fundraising campaign. I think that kind of work is just great. Am I interrupting anything, do you have a moment to talk?" I pulled into a parking lot in order to give David my full attention.

He went on to explain that he was the founder of a foundation called 'Ironheart'. He explained that the foundation served as a campaign that raised awareness for racers that suffered from heart disease or other cardiac conditions. He then opened up about his personal life way more than I could have expected. "I actually can relate to racers with heart conditions; I have also gone through the process of an open-heart surgery. In fact, I technically died on the operating table, and they had to bring me back. So here I am today, working to raise awareness about racers that have gone through similar situations to defy the odds and stand out as role models in their community." Hearing this, I decided to divulge personal information of my own story and experience. After having a heart-to-heart with this person who just minutes ago was a complete stranger, I felt a close connection to David, much like how I had felt with Bill from Ironman. He could relate on every level to what I had been through, as well as all of the checks and balances and daily medicine I had to go through. I wanted to get involved with the foundation, knowing that this was the next step for me. I just knew that this foundation and this cause was what it was all about.

David explained that the idea of membership in the foundation was to organize fundraisers and campaigns to educate people about heart conditions some athletes face; these funds were then used to help people gain access to appointments, procedures and medicines they would otherwise go without. The foundation was still in its infancy, and only a handful of people were involved so far. However, David was planning an advertising blitz soon and expected the foundation to grow both in influence and size.

And grow it did. Just after I agreed to join the cause, Ironheart started taking off. An Ironheart 5k road race was slated to benefit the foundation in Concord, and the community embraced the event. This public setting allowed us to get information out into the community on a large scale like we couldn't do otherwise. I could tell the foundation was poised to become a powerful entity in the future.

In 2011, David contacted me, giddy with excitement and saying he wanted to run an awesome idea by me. "I want to take six or seven cardiac athletes, film them for one full year and make a movie or documentary about it, titled 'Flat Line to Finish Line,'" he explained. I liked the idea, but had several questions.

"It sounds pretty cool. But how are you going to coordinate all of that? They'd all be doing different things and might even be in different parts of the world. And what would you film? Their lives, races they did?"

"I'm glad you asked. I was thinking that we would all train together. For a year. And at the end of that year, we would do an Ironman."

I did not see that coming, and was speechless for a while after David threw out the idea. I was flashing back to different moments from my Ironman race a year ago. All of the training and hard work that had gone into competing, not to mention the difficulty of the race itself, flooded back into my mind. Also, the struggle of juggling home life and intense training all over again was not exactly a welcome thought. I was hesitant to agree to go through all of that again. On the other hand, Ironman had been nothing short of life-changing. Why not experience that all over again? But then there was the time and commitment factor that Ironman training demanded. All of these thoughts were quarreling with one another at the same time.

In the end, I knew I had to do it. The idea was great, and it was something I dearly wanted to be a part of. I told David I was in. Excited that I was on board, David promised to get me information soon regarding dates and times for the whole project.

There was one problem that I hadn't foreseen when I signed up for this project: telling Brook what I would be doing. The minute that I realized I needed to break the news to her, I got what I call the "….crap" feeling. I closed my eyes and shook my head, knowing this would not be the most welcome piece of news in the household. Two weeks passed between the initial conversation with David and the point that I finally got the nerve to tell Brook.

We were both on lunch break from work and were sitting in a parking lot after eating. I told her everything David had told me, adding in that this would have even more of an impact than my first Ironman. He had sent me dates and times for the preliminary gatherings and training sessions since our talk, so I also gave Brook that information. She sat patiently, listening to every word I said and looking calmly over the schedule I handed her. Then I gave her some specific information about the process of filming the documentary. When training, we would have sports cameras on helmets to get real-time first-person video of our perspective. As for the personal end of the project, a camera crew would be coming to our respective home towns and filming everything we did for two to three days.

"Wait, you mean they'll be here all the time? Constantly, 24/7, in this house? Do I have to talk on camera?" Brook asked, alarmed.

"Not 24/7, but most of the day. And yes, in the house. The idea is to get a picture of our daily lives to couple with our training."

"Jeez, that means I need to clean the house and fix up things around here. We have a lot to work out before they're here." Brook was clearly stressed about the idea of a filming crew in the house. After I finished, there was a silence between us while I awaited her response. She made me sweat it out before answering. She was well along in her pregnancy with our second child at this time, and this had certainly factored into my decision.

"Okay Jeremy, how about this: I'm okay with you doing this project. However, here's the deal. Bryn is due November second. This says you're flying out to Arizona to sign up for Ironman around November fifteenth. If Bryn is even one day late, you are not going, I don't feel comfortable with you being gone for as long as this says you will be if Bryn is late." That was completely fair. Brook had been unbelievably supportive when I had trained for Ironman last time and never gave me too much of a hard time about Daddy duty. So her asking for this one condition was completely fine, I wasn't about to argue that at all.

As it turned out, Bryn actually came early. She was born without any complications, and Brook and I were overjoyed. Even Ellie was excited to meet her little sister. It was one of the most heartwarming moments of my life to witness Ellie meeting Bryn for the first time. Ellie was all smiles and waved to Bryn, and I watched with a tear in my eye.

As much as I was excited to meet up with the movie crew and David and get the project going, I was reluctant to leave the newest member of our perfect family. I knew that I'd be back soon though, and Brook assured me that she had a handle on things. With a bunch of goodbye kisses and hugs, along with a 'Daddy will be home soon from his trip' to Ellie, I left the house to meet up with David at the airport.

I hopped on a bus from Manchester, New Hampshire to Logan Airport in Boston. From there, I took a flight from Boston to Phoenix, Arizona. The 2011 Ironman race was to be held there. We were scheduled to be in Arizona for five days of filming and volunteering. It started off with meeting all of the athletes that would be in the documentary. We lived all over the country, so none of us had met each other before, except for the exchanges we had over several previous conference calls. In fact, the four months leading up to this trip was filled with calls from David, my fellow athletes, and other members of the Ironheart Foundation.

David is our fearless leader. Not only was he the brains of the project, but he was a cast member as well. He is the mind that set Ironheart in motion. He has two daughters, which stirred lots of conversations and story swapping. We could both relate to our family structures; being outnumbered by the girls. I look up to all of the accomplishments David has achieved and everything he has done in his life. He is certainly on the path to changing lots of lives with his work.

The first athlete (aside from David) I met that would be featured in "Flat Line to Finish Line" was Scott Roy, a respected coach and accomplished triathlete from Washington. He was the closest to me in age out of the whole cast. Even though we hadn't met in person before Arizona, we already knew each other very well. After our preliminary conference calls ended, we continued talking to each other in a separate call. It was much the same situation as Bill from my first Ironman race; even though we had only talked here and there, I felt a strong connection with Scott.

I immediately noticed his charismatic personality and constant smile. We quickly struck up long conversations about everything; family, fitness, training, and life overall. He told me about how he had run Ironman last year and run with an athlete that he knew was having trouble, sacrificing a fast time on the marathon to help a newer athlete push through. This story really shows the true personality and good nature of Scott that I grew to know over my time in Arizona.

Just like Scott, all of my fellow athletes were great, inspirational individuals. For the first time, my situation was not a unique one. These guys could relate to what I had been through. It was so moving to be able to work with these amazing people, and to know that I was considered to be on the same level as these incredible athletes was an honor.

Jim Oldfield was the oldest member of the cast; you'd think he was the father of the group, and he was in a way. He always looked out for the well-being of the whole cast when we would train together. When I first met Jim, I instantly got the vibe that he was one of those people that loves something so much that he wants to do it until he can't do anything at all, and his something is triathlons.

Adam Knight was the youngest of the cast and the newest to the triathlon scene. He was a very down-to-earth individual that loved what we were doing in Arizona and was proud to be a part of it. Whatever he did, he never put anything less than all he had. Whether it was an early morning run or a short interview, he left everything on the table. This made it really fun to work with him during our training and filming.

Ellen Charnley was the toughest member of the cast, hands down. She had a chiseled physique and loved fitness of all kinds. Her smile always lit up the entire room or area, the kind of infectious smile that makes you smile in response. She's married with no kids, and the whole cast grew to love her husband, who was always offering encouragement. Ellen shared with us that she had just written a book on her experiences with racing and her heart condition. I loved the idea, promising myself that I would do the same one day. I mean, how hard could it be?

Patrick Hight was one of those people that never got old. Even though his kids were already adults, he was still young at heart. At 52 years young, Patrick was doing many incredible things in his community with the Ironheart Foundation. He always held great conversations, which were only made more enjoyable with his southern accent.

Ryan Leong was a phenomenal athlete that had raced in his share of elite races, such as the Ironman World Championships. He was a superb person to be around and had a great outlook on life. His wife was one of the biggest supporters on the initial trip down to Arizona and kept everybody smiling.

We checked in for volunteering at the race first thing, then got ourselves situated at the hotel. When we weren't meeting people important to the foundation, we were busy with filming or training. The days were crazy. We always woke up at four or five in the morning, and didn't get to bed until late in the night. Lots of filming was done in such a short amount of time. Multiple interviews were conducted for each athlete, with most of the personal interviews filmed during our stay. We had a couple of dinners together with the whole cast and crew, otherwise we were allowed to go and do our own thing.

Then came the volunteering for Ironman. As usual, the experience was amazing. Words can't do Ironman justice. Having raced in Ironman now gave me a whole different perspective on volunteering. I was more involved and more efficient than the last time I had volunteered at Lake Placid. Looking back at how far I had come and how much had changed over those few years was crazy. Last time I had volunteered, I wasn't a father. Now I was the proud parent of two beautiful girls. I hadn't experienced the event myself when I volunteered the first time. Now I was an Ironman and having a documentary made about my life experiences and my training for my second Ironman race.

After many long hours of filming, interviewing and volunteering, our week in Arizona came to an end. I said my goodbyes to the cast members and the crew that I had grown close to over the week and grabbed a red-eye flight home. As much as I tried, I got no sleep on the flight. No position was comfortable, and I was restless. When the plane landed in Boston, I was completely exhausted. I practically had to tape my eyes open for the bus ride home from the airport.

Brook was waiting for me at the door when I pulled into the driveway. I rubbed my eyes as I shut the car off, hoping that I didn't look too drained. She handed Bryn to me the moment I got inside. "Welcome home, your turn!" she said.

"Hun, I really need to get some sleep. I got none on the plane and I'm exhausted."

"That makes two of us Jeremy, but go for it," she said. I could sense the exasperation in her tone. I felt bad, and it was obvious that I wasn't the most popular person in the house. I sat down on the couch and passed out in seconds. Apparently my mother stopped by and talked to me, but I have no recollection of this. After grabbing three hours of mediocre sleep, I was woken up by Ellie playing in the living room. She saw me stretch and ran over for a hug. She was excited to see me and asked about my trip. I told her about all that I had done as she played with her toys. I went over to Bryn and held her; I had missed her dearly while in Arizona, and it felt so good to be holding her again. She was now almost three weeks old and growing fast. I knew that Brook really needed a break from managing the household single-handedly, so I forced myself awake and let her know I had a handle on things. She didn't need to hear any more, and made her way up to our room for some well-deserved rest.

The first few days after getting home from filming were a blur. I found myself reflecting on how quickly everything had changed. I had to ask myself several times if Arizona had really occurred. Being a part of this documentary was a huge step for everything. My training was back up to Ironman levels and my story was being told for everyone to see. In the past several years, I had become an Ironman and father. While I wasn't complaining, so much had evolved in my life in a short span of five years.

The new year of 2012 rolled in, and so did another conference call from David. There had been very little contact over the previous six weeks, but this call assured me that the documentary was still very much on. It started with a quick recap of the content and experiences covered at Ironman six weeks prior. David then detailed the agenda for the rest of the project. The expectations of us as the cast were laid out and each of us were told what we were going to be working on individually.

Filming would encompass the next nine months, and culminate with the Ironman race in Arizona in the fall. Any major life events along the way would also be documented. However, David did not want the crew recording these. Instead, he wanted amateur video of these, possibly filmed by family or friends. This, he said, would capture the real individual feel that would separate this documentary from others. "I want to bring the true essence of your lives to the screen, and this is how we will do that," he explained.

The rest of the project started immediately after that conference call ended. From that point on, anything in my life and training was fair game. I would wear a sports camera every now and then during training. Any significant life event (move, new job, family event) was to be recorded and catalogued. These life events would serve as supplemental material to the main body of the documentary: our training for Ironman. Most of the filming of this project had revolved around the physical aspect, this quickly changed.

Late in April of 2012, I got a phone call with devastating news. A choked-up David told me that Scott had passed away at his home in Washington. I was leveled, shocked. Those words hit harder than a sucker punch in the gut. He was the first athlete I had met in Arizona. David told me that Scott had gone out for a routine bike ride, come home, and suddenly collapsed. He was only 38 years old and still in his athletic prime. This news hurt not only me but the entire documentary team, cast and crew alike.

The news of Scott's passing quickly spread. We all decided to set up our own conference call with one another. We were all so taken aback at Scott's death. It was apparent that this man had had a major impact on every one of us. This news caused lots of self-evaluation and doubt among all of us. David thought out loud, asking, "What are we really doing here, everyone? Are we being reckless? Are we pushing our limits farther than we should be?" He had been closer to Scott than any of us, and the news of Scott's passing had him reeling.

Everyone was distraught. I was seriously questioning my actions, both past and present. I had gone through two open-heart surgeries in a ten-year span and now I was training for a second go at one of the most demanding races the world has to offer. Was that really smart? Are these training plans going to push me over my limit? This project had quickly turned from a documentary on Ironman training to something much, much bigger. Now, this film was really, truly about survival and combating adversity. We came to the consensus that despite this tragedy, we were going to press on, agreeing that Scott would scoff at the idea of us stopping this project. David wrapped up that conversation by saying definitively, "We have to tell his story. It's an amazing one, and if anyone deserves their story told, it's Scott."

To further cement this decision, his wife joined forces as a cast member and started training for Ironman in Scott's honor. The company that runs Ironman was contacted about the situation regarding Scott and his wife. She made the request that she not only be allowed to run in his stead, but also that she could wear his race number on that day. The company obliged without hesitation, offering their deepest condolences. I have the highest respect for Scott's wife and what she did that year in his memory. The way she kept his legacy moving forward was something that none of us will ever forget.

Adversity reared its ugly head again not long after Scott's passing. Jim, one of our oldest cast members, was set to run Ironman alongside his son. One day, Jim got the call a parent never wants to get: he was told that his son was in the hospital and clinging to life. We were later told that Jim's son had been driving to a race with his girlfriend when he was hit by a drunk driver. The accident was horrific, and Jim's son was med-flighted to a hospital. Through a strong display of willpower, his son survived the crash and has since recovered thanks to surgery and months of rehabilitation. At the time that it happened, however, we were all shaken up yet again. This documentary that was supposed to be focused on simple training had turned into something totally different than intended. One of our cast members had passed away and another was bedside in a hospital while his son was fighting for his life.

These two events forced us to see that even though we were all elite athletes, we were still human. Our abilities to perform as we could were a gift, and we all wanted to do as much with these abilities as possible. We all let these thoughts settle over the next month. We all kept up with our rigorous training through the summer. At the end of the summer we held a conference call and discussed where we all were, both physically and mentally. We were all on the same page with our training. Though we were still shaken from the events that transpired over the past few months, we again came to the decision to grind for it. This was too real not to keep going.

Shortly before heading back out to Arizona, I started getting into the more intensive training for Ironman. The peak training would be done in Arizona with the rest of the cast. This is not to say the training just before the peak training is easy. I was covering hundreds of miles per week through my training, which is nothing to scoff at. Five weeks before leaving for Arizona I had my annual echo appointment. This had been my final medical clearance for my previous Ironman in 2010, and would serve the same purpose this year. I felt great during training and went into the appointment confident that I would get the green light to race.

The film crew for the documentary accompanied me to the check-up, since this echocardiogram was certainly a major part of maintaining my well-being. I checked in at the hospital, filled out the usual paperwork and greeted the cardiologist. The echo went off without a hitch, along with other simple measurements that were taken to ensure my heart was performing as it should. The doctor jotted information down from his work, and then left the room for several minutes as he usually did. He then came back in the room to give me the diagnosis.

"Well, Jeremy, I don't have good or bad news, but just news in general. How you take it is your call entirely. There was a change in your echo from last year. There has been an enlargement in your aorta." I got a nervous, sinking feeling as I heard this. "Now you'll probably be fine to do Ironman, but I personally would not do it if I was in your shoes. On the other hand, you've overcome some ridiculous odds in the past, which is why I say this is entirely in your hands as to whether you want to go through with racing. You can do it, but I wouldn't suggest it. That's all I'm going to say; the final call is up to you."

As devastated by this news as I was, the decision was a no-brainer. My options were to disregard the advice of a medical professional and go into the peak training for the race, or opt out and simply support the film crew. I had already finished an Ironman race and I wasn't about to roll the dice with my health and well-being for the sake of doing it again. It only took a brief thought of my girls for me to know that this was something I needed to sit out. The thought of an unforeseen accident happening because of my negligence that would make it so I wouldn't be able to provide for them was unbearable.

I was bummed because I had trained for almost a year for Ironman and now would not be participating directly in the race, but I wasn't going to risk ending up with a bad situation from overworking myself. I had seen first-hand that accidents could happen even from not overexerting oneself and wasn't about to go against a sound medical opinion.

Hearing this medical advice brought a very real element to my journey. I got home and hugged all of my girls tightly before breaking the news to Brook. She understood that I was upset with the outcome of the echo and was glad that I had come to the conclusion to not race. I started winding down my training, seeing as I would be going to Arizona as a supporter rather than a participant. I passed the news on to David and my fellow cast members, all of whom were very supportive and optimistic about my decision. I learned that Adam had also not received the green light to race, and that he would be assisting the camera crew with filming on the big day. Hearing the outpouring of support from the rest of the cast lightened my spirits and put a positive spin on the situation.

Then came November and our big return to Ironman, on one level or another. We all reunited in Arizona almost a year after our initial meeting. So much had changed for all of us in that time span. We were short one of our original cast members, but his wife was continuing his journey. There were some truly amazing sections filmed when we first arrived in Arizona. Scott's son, Reese, had flown down to support his mother and to honor his father. The entire cast and crew made the call to have Reese lead us on a run for the first scene of the trip. Reese accepted the offer without hesitation. This moment was touching for everyone involved. Personally, it is a moment that I will never forget; one of the most moving of the entire experience of the documentary, in my opinion.

We did a lot more interviews before the big race. Many of these interviews linked with the interviews that we had done at Ironman in 2011 and served as a follow-up to the previous clips. In between these and group training sessions, David and the crew would often gather us to explain what some of the procedures and logistics would be during the race. He would gather us after a group run or swim and go over where the camera crews would be during that section of the race. For example, film crews would be on motorcycles during the bike ride portion of the race. Several crewmembers would be hovering over the water during the swim and filming from a helicopter.

Based on these talks, I really appreciated the amount of people involved in getting the footage needed for the film. There were at least ten people in the camera crew, and they were doing a lot more than just standing in one spot with a tripod. They had to move as we moved. I can't imagine that filming from a motorcycle is all that easy, especially with professional-grade camera equipment. So many people were donating their time to make this documentary happen, and I made it a point to thank each one of them, much in the same way I did for volunteers during my Ironman race in 2010.

The day before the race, Ellen came down with a nasty case of food poisoning. She had an IV in her arm to deliver medicine a mere ten hours before the race was to start. But, proving how tough she really is, she combated both dehydration and her sickness to race.

Race morning brought loads of interviews and comments for the media and press, along with filming of everything by the film crew. I searched the crowd for four of my friends from back home that were racing that day and wished them good luck on the course. One of my friends from home was Marc Dupuis. He would not be racing that day; instead, he was the unofficial chiropractor for team Ironheart. He made sure that our entire cast was as aligned as possible for the race. He and I would be volunteering together for the duration of the race, an experience I was looking forward to.

The process of assisting our team and volunteering with the race was just as rewarding as my previous experience. It was odd that I had a plan to race and was neck-deep in my training and now I was doing something other than racing at Ironman, but I was able to still be a part of the whole experience. The entire experience that year was a great one, and cheering on my teammates during their race was amazing. Jim had a hard time during the race, but I did everything I could to boost his confidence and energy for his time out on the course.

Overall, the feel at Ironman is one of a close-knit community.

Racers come from all over the world, but when racing in Ironman, I've felt like I'm racing with 2,500 close friends. This sport creates not only a community feel, but that of a family. While there are no positions or teams as in other sports, triathlons have a funny way of bringing the participants close together.

After experiencing Ironman and other races as many times as I had, I realized how much I loved the sport of triathlon. I knew that someday I wanted to coach the sport, as Sean had done for me when I was starting out. The first step to reaching this goal was to get a coaching certification, similar to a certification needed to be a fitness trainer. I made up my mind to pursue this certification and my goal of becoming a triathlon coach.

In the meantime, I made my way home from Ironman, but not before wishing each one of my fellow cast members a safe trip home and good luck in their future endeavors. I would miss every one of them, including the camera crew. But I knew I wanted to get home and make a difference in my hometown.

Since volunteering in Arizona, I have put on several road races in my community to benefit the Ironheart Foundation. Through a couple of 5k runs and several one-mile events, we have been able to raise enough money to not only benefit the foundation but also to benefit our local community. This is the goal that I feel everyone should aim for; to be able to give back to the community that they call their home. And this goal is never ending. I am always looking for bigger, better and more innovative ways to benefit my community.

Since Ironman Arizona, I have earned my certification as a USAT (USA Triathlon) Coach. Not only that, but I have taken it one step further and become a USAT race director, along with earning the requisite certification. I feel that triathlon events, when correctly implemented, have the ability to produce a massive positive change in a community.

The cohesiveness that can result from triathlon sports is immense, and I only hope that I can continue to make that difference made through this awesome sport.

Chapter Seventeen
The Female Woodwards

Through everything I have done and experienced in my adult life, my girls have been at the center of it all; not only Ellie, Bryn and Isla, but also (and especially) my wife. Everything revolves around my family. Despite all of my experiences and projects, I have made sure that my number one priority is to be there for my daughters and wife. I don't want to miss anything, and have had to work tirelessly to ensure that is the case. My girls have grown to be the most amazing kids in existence, and I couldn't ask for a better wife.

From the first point that Brook and I knew we were going to be parents, we knew that we wanted Brook to stay home with our daughter. While I have the utmost respect for babysitters and nannies and the incredible work they do, we wanted to experience all the milestones with our child. Right from the start, Ellie was an easy baby. She cried just as much as any other newborn, but she slept soundly through the nights, unlike most other newborns. The first night back from the hospital after she was born, she slept way longer than we were expecting. Not only that, but Brook and I woke well-rested, a pleasant surprise.

We dove into parenting with the expectation that we would be sleep-deprived for a significant amount of time, and have no down time. On the contrary, Brook always told me when I got home from work that Ellie had been very manageable. We were in disbelief. We had plenty of time for rest and relaxation and all three of us slept soundly on a regular basis.

On our second daughter's first night home, we had the same expectations we had had for Ellie; we'd be up through the entire night and get next to no sleep. However, our daughters continued to prove us wrong, as Bryn slept a solid six hours during her first night home. "This is awesome!" I said to Brook. We were two for two on the excellent sleeping patterns with our kids.

We quickly learned that was not to continue. That first night home may be the only night in Bryn's three years with us that she has slept for six hours. On the nights that she would cry and scream excessively, Brook and I would exchange worried glances with one another, weighing options to try that might help Bryn sleep more soundly. Nowadays, Bryn and Ellie sleep better, but we still have yet to have both of them regularly sleeping through an entire night.

In 2016, we found out that Bryn would no longer be the youngest, with another baby girl due in April of 2017. In December of 2016, we moved into a new house, and with my wife closing in on her third trimester, moving while juggling two sparkling bundles of energy was stressful. I had to ensure the girls multiple times that Santa had our new address and he knew where to deliver all of their gifts. Once all the moving boxes were in the appropriate rooms, I sprang the news on my wife that we were going to have the governor over for dinner in a week, which would fall three days after Christmas. I only ended up spending two nights on the couch for that.

As Brook's due date approached, which happened to be Marathon Monday, the plans to run the Boston Marathon were up in the air. However, Isla Woodward ensured that wouldn't be an issue, storming into the world on March 30th.

She has such a bright personality and brings laughter to our entire family. Isla has my temperament, which can be good and bad in the body of a toddler. Whenever she gets in need of a nap, I can lay her down on my chest and she falls asleep instantly, drifting off to the click of my heart valve. She is an amusing mix of both of her older sisters.

Bryn wants to be just like her older sister. As a father, this is the cutest thing I could imagine. Whatever Ellie is playing with, Bryn wants to join in. Ellie is working on a page in a coloring book? Bryn's right there getting going on the adjacent page. Lego towers are built by our two little engineers on a regular basis. They are both so much fun to be around, and they both have amazing little personalities. Even though they're both still very young, their personalities are far ahead of their physical growth. Even though they are very similar with their interests, their personalities are what really differentiate these two. Without question, Bryn is the daredevil child. This is not to say that Ellie doesn't get into her fair share of hairy situations, but Bryn is certainly the frontrunner - Brook and I really need to keep an eye on her when she gets older. We've joked that we are eventually going to get the call of, "Yes, Mr. Woodward, your daughter hurt herself doing crazy flips off of a bridge into the river, could you come get her?"

In our household, I have become completely outnumbered. The girls have overrun the entire house, and I've had to fight to keep any Jeremy-only space, with little success. From the point that Ellie was old enough to enjoy toys, the house gradually transformed into a pink-splattered, toy-covered area. I accepted this and knew it would happen. In preparation, I had quarantined certain areas for myself that I tried to keep girl-proof.

This venture proved to be a failure as Ellie and Bryn slowly took over each space one by one. Soon I was left with just one Jeremy-only space throughout the house. I had just been evicted from my second-to-last fortress by a horde of glitter and toys. My last hiding spot was downstairs in the basement and served as my think chamber. The corner doubled as my martial arts shrine, with diplomas, belts and awards covering the wall. This was my last bit of real estate in the Woodward household and I wanted to keep it as my area for when I needed a bit of solitary time, work-related thought, relaxation with a book, or even just to have some peace and quiet.

Just a week after being evicted from my second to last fortress, I came home to a sparkly work station downstairs. I chuckled at how the tables had turned on me so quickly, and wondered what the girls would do from here, now that they had made it clear that their presence was needed everywhere in the house.

I made my office upstairs in the attic as my man cave, moving my martial arts collection into the corner office and adorning the walls with triathlon-themed newspaper articles and magazine spreads. I dreamed that one day I would have my own fitness gym, and jokingly thought that it could be the ultimate equivalent of a man cave.

When I did Ironman in 2010, seeing Ellie in the crowd all the time was so much fun. I would see her at one transition with my mother, and by the next transition Brook was holding her. After that, my Dad would be holding her high over the crowd so I could see her. At the end of the race, she wanted an Ironman t-shirt. We got it the day after the race for her, and she loved it. She wore it proudly as much as we would let her, and often protested when we had to wash it. The shirt had the Ironman symbol emblazoned on the front, along with 'my Daddy is faster than your Daddy' on the back.

Both Ellie and Bryn have said that they want to do triathlons one day. Every now and then, one or both of them will run with me for a little bit during a morning run, or pedal their training bikes next to mine as I do several laps around the local park. They even know triathlon terminology, throwing terms like 'cut off' or 'transition' into their little conversations with one another. They really like being a part of my training and being included in what I do, and it warms my heart to see.

One thing that both Ellie and Bryn have fallen in love with already is dance. My mother has owned a dance studio for over forty years, so they love having her as both a grandmother and a dance coach. Bryn was the youngest student my mother has ever taught. At eight months of age, Bryn could already walk around on the stage with my mother's help. As for Ellie, she is now seven years old and in her fourth year of dance. She has become so good that she is a teacher's assistant for my mother during some of the younger kids' classes. During some classes, Ellie will actually teach Bryn.

Like everything else, Bryn wants to be just like Ellie in dance. She tries to replicate Ellie's routines and mannerisms during classes at the dance studio, and it's the cutest thing. Seeing that Ellie is such a good role model for her sister is the greatest feeling. And then to see Bryn striving to be just like Ellie is even better.

When Ellie was first born, Brook and I knew we wanted to get her involved in sports when the time came. However, we did not want to overschedule her, and the same mentality went for Bryn. Luckily we haven't had to worry about that issue, because all Ellie and Bryn want to do is dance. As a father, seeing this degree of dedication at their early ages is so cool.

Growing up in a household with a dance studio owner for a mother, everybody thought that I danced as well. This is not the case at all. I did do some gymnastics early on, but that was simply to learn how to tumble and learn some basic flips. I'm that guy that when I go to a wedding, I do everything possible to avoid the dance floor, something that drives my wife (and my mother) crazy. They always wanted me to be more into dancing, but I could never get into it.

That all changed in 2013. I was contacted by a representative from a local technical college. She was running a fundraiser for the school titled 'Concord Stars' that aimed to gather familiar local faces and have them pair up, work on a dance routine and then face off in a competition. The funds raised would go to the college. I had caught wind of the fundraiser before. It was in its infancy, as this would be the third year it had been held. I liked the idea, and the representative sold me on the part with a 'good way to represent community' talk.

I decided to go for it, despite knowing that it was way out of my comfort zone and that it would be a challenge. I would be dancing with a colleague of mine named Erin. We had twelve weeks to practice before the event. When I told Brook what I would be undertaking for the next three months, she looked at me and laughed. "What? You, dance? You never dance." I explained to her the fundraising aspect, and she nodded in acknowledgement. "So after this, you better be able to dance whenever we go out," she said, sounding more serious than joking.

Erin and I practiced a few hours each week prior to the event. We wanted more time to practice, but our conflicting work schedules didn't allow it. To make our routine the best it could possibly be, my mother served as our coach. The minute she heard that I was working on a dance routine for a friendly competition, she was on board. She is fiercely competitive as a coach. Add that to the fact that she is my mother and the result was that she pushed me almost as hard as my karate instructor does during our practice times. In a way, dancing is similar to the forms portion of martial arts; both are a prescribed set of moves and both can be done with different flare depending on the person. My mother knew this, and pushed me even more because of it. "Since I'm helping you put this together, you had better win this, Jeremy. Otherwise, there's going to be some uncomfortable dinners for a few weeks after when you come over on Sunday nights," she scolded.

Every time I would leave for practice, our girls would laugh.

"Daddy's going to dance? But you don't dance, Daddy," Ellie said, perplexed.

"I know Ellie, you're right. He doesn't," Brook would reply sarcastically with a light-hearted smirk and a playful glance.

After what felt like a lot less than twelve weeks, the gym at the college was transformed into a ballroom and it was time for the big performance. I learned that the event was sold out that year, and that the gym would be packed with six hundred spectators. My friends joked that people were coming to see me mess up and fail horribly, but I knew that Erin and I had a formidable routine ready to go. When our turn came, we strutted out confidently onto the dance floor and completely crushed our routine. We hit every pose, every move and didn't mess up any aspect.

The whole place went nuts when we finished our dance. I was completely out of breath, but had just had so much fun with our dance. I looked at Brook and beamed. She was standing and clapping over her head, telling me later she had no idea I could move like that. Erin and I ended up winning both the 'people's choice' award and 'best overall routine', both of which were the top honors for the night. To this day, my girls always remind me of my run-in with dancing from that event. On a side note, there were no issues with Sunday dinners at Mom's thanks to our performance.

Both Ellie and Bryn enjoy going to our events and races. If I'm running an event, my two girls are my assistants throughout the entire time. If Brook is running a race, one of them is on my shoulders waving to her while the other jumps up and down. Brook and I also feel that it's important for them to see us being physically involved, as this will instill good physical habits for them in the future. Ellie has even shadowed me at work, following my every move and even carrying a stopwatch just like I do when I coach.

One moment with my girls that I will never forget was in the late spring of 2014. Brook was going to be running a 5k race later in the day. I had to go in and teach a class at work before heading over to support her. I walked through the living room and let my girls know I was going to teach class and that I'd be back right after so Brook could head to the course and warm up before running. I went to work, taught my class and hustled home to grab Ellie and Bryn. Brook headed out the minute I walked in, giving me a quick kiss in passing.

When the three of us got to the course, Ellie kept saying that she wanted to run the 5k with Brook. I kept trying to explain to her that we weren't there to run, but to cheer on their mother. "But I wanna run wiff Mommy!" Ellie protested. Brook heard this as she walked over.

"We could. Do you really want to, Ellie? It's a long way, your legs will be tired by the end," Brook explained to Ellie in her soothing motherly way. Ellie asked how Bryn would be with us, and Brook answered that she would push Bryn in her stroller. That settled it; the entire Woodward clan would be running the 5k that day.

To our amazement, Ellie ran almost the entire time. There were many quick walking breaks, but then she was right back to running right next to Brook. We were one of the last to finish the race, but Ellie ran across the finish line with her arms outstretched, palms turned upward with an ear-to-ear grin. Her joy didn't end with the race, because the 5k was all Ellie talked about for a good two weeks. Seeing how happy Ellie was to finish her first 5k race (at age six, no less) was spectacular. The fact that she included her little sister in the beginning was perfect.

Bryn has certainly had her moments as well. Just after she was born, I got a tattoo on my right forearm of both of my daughters' names. When she was old enough to know that her name was on my arm, she thought it was hilarious. "Can you wash it off, Daddy?" I told her I couldn't and gave her a simple explanation of how it was permanent. For some reason, Bryn thought that me having her name on my arm was hysterical and kept laughing about it, pointing it out to Brook and laughing even more.

One thing that is always interesting in our household is family movie time. The girls love their animated movies, and by love, I mean 'will watch over and over and over again'. I cannot count the number of times that we have watched certain movies at this point. In 2013, Ellie and Bryn fell in love with a hit movie that had just come out, and were prancing around the house singing the soundtrack so much that I memorized it just from listening to them. The movie's plot revolved around sisters, so of course they acted out some scenes with one another from time to time. They both were so hooked on the movie that Ellie decided to sing the movies hit song at a dance recital on stage during Bryn's dance. Them being on stage together and performing at the same time is the most adorable thing anyone could ever imagine. I was melting in my chair watching it, so much that I wanted to run up on stage and pull both of them into the biggest hug. That performance is a shining moment in their lives so far.

I joke that I have three little girls in the house; I just happen to be a father to two of them and a husband to the other. In reality, Brook is a stupendous person in every aspect imaginable. She makes sure that I'm aware of the priorities at all times, and definitely keeps me in check. In other words, she calls me out when I'm being a moron. She also doesn't let me get away with anything. "Yeah yeah yeah, you just ran a 5k for the community and it was a great success, now go take out the trash," is just an example of the jiving relationship we have. She is not only my wife, but my best friend. We can give each other lip and know that we're just messing with one another. This, to me, is the sign of a great relationship.

Everything Brook does is for the family, regardless of how big or small. She makes lunches for the girls for school, gets them to dance practice and play dates, and takes care of us when we're sick. While I do the majority of the work outside of the home, Brook certainly has the harder task of being a stay-at-home mother. Anyone that says a stay-at-home parent has the easier job would get an earful from my wife. Through all of the obstacles and challenges we have faced from every angle, she has done beautifully, all the while being an amazing mother to our children.

Despite the fact that she is a miracle worker, there is one thing that Brook really doesn't like: being in the spotlight. So in 2010, when my wife and I were invited to have lunch with the Governor and his wife at the state office, Brook was not too fond of the idea. We were invited due to my fundraising events I had set up through the Nature Conservancy for my Ironman race. I was excited, but Brook was nervous beyond belief. "Why do you put me through this kind of torture?!" she complained when I told her about the plan. She paraded around the house, running her own marathon between the closet and bathroom. Finally when she was satisfied with how she looked, we headed to the state house for lunch. In the end, it was amazing and a great experience.

With Brook, she is either all into something or not interested at all, and there is no in between. In January of 2013, she approached me and said something I had been waiting to hear for a long time. "You know, Jeremy, I want to try something new, I need a new experience. I want to do a triathlon." I was more amped up with excitement than any kid in a candy store has ever been. I instantly started putting together a training program for her.

Brook already did training sessions with me and yoga classes elsewhere, so she didn't have to work terribly hard to prepare for the sprint-distance triathlon that she would be doing. She prepared for the race perfectly, following every step of the training to the letter. In the house, the racing attention from Ellie and Bryn started to shift from "daddy raced here, daddy biked there" to "Mommy's going triathlon!"

This was a huge step for Brook. Doing a sprint-distance triathlon was way out of her comfort zone. She trained with full commitment and effort up until the day before the race, when he headed down to a hotel for the night. She went to bed the minute we got there in order to be as ready as possible for the race.

We woke up at 3:30 in the morning well rested and ready to take on the day. I would not be racing alongside my wife, but would serve as the lead cheerleader for her with Ellie and Bryn. Brook was stressing out about how to get the girls up and into the car without having them cry in protest the whole way. I told her I had it under control and got the girls buckled into their car seats. To my relief, they were as happy as could be during the ride to the venue. On the way to the race Brook was really nervous, voicing concerns that she'd have a lapse in focus during the race and mess up somehow. I assured her that she would do great and that she had nothing to worry about. The girls joined in, telling Brook about how good she would do that day, which brightened her spirits tremendously.

Brook did excellent throughout the entire race. My daughters and I had made little signs before the race to hold up for Brook, and we waved them as she ran through the different transition areas. We even got a great spot in the crowd at the finish line and cheered Brook on as she finished her first triathlon. She ran across the finish line, beaming when she saw our homemade signs. I had planned a party for her that night at my parent's house to celebrate her success. Her friends had managed to keep the secret, and she was completely surprised at the turnout. I was bursting at the seams with pride at what my wife had accomplished. She had been apprehensive when first starting the training, a bundle of nerves at the starting line, but had jogged across the finish with an air of confidence. That day, she showed how amazing a woman she really is.

My girls mean the world to me. My daughters enrich my life like

I never thought possible. Being involved in my daughters' lives is my number one priority. Having them take part in dancing classes with my mother as their coach instills in them the value of family. They love what they do, and that to me is the most important part. We could have them in multiple sports and ferry them left and right, but they are completely happy with focusing on dance. My wife is the most supportive and caring woman I have ever met. Brook is the best person I have ever met and I am so lucky to have her as the mother to our children. My girls have taught me that no matter what the variables are that life throws at you, regardless of anything else in life, if your family is where your priorities lie, then life is good.

Chapter Eighteen
When Life Gives You Lessons, Heed Them

Anything is possible. Anything can be accomplished. These are the two main takeaways I've had throughout life. During all of my treatments for my heart condition, I had doctors and others telling me that I couldn't do this, I wouldn't be able to do that. While I obviously respect the opinions of the doctors, as they're doing their job, I've made a life out of doing exactly what people said I couldn't do. Without a winning attitude, nothing can fall into place. But with a winning attitude, positive outlook and a solid work ethic, amazing things that seemed like far-off hopes will soon turn into goals. These goals will then become benchmarks, and from there achievements.

We all have the ability to inspire others. I believe that we all have a responsibility to do just that. Also, how one person will inspire others is different from any other person. Good parenting inspires the children of those parents. Good teachers inspire their students. As a fitness and triathlon coach, I push myself and hope that I leave work that day having inspired my clients.

There are many different ways to inspire and be inspired. The takeaway thought with this is that so many people have served as inspirational role models to each one of us. Just as we have taken life lessons from each of these figures and applied them to our own lives, we will pass these onto the next generation. All of us, have, are, and will be inspirations to others in our lives. Whether it be through direct interaction or simply setting a great social example, we are always leaving positive imprints on the lives of others. The more conscious of this fact we are, the more of an impact we can leave.

In my gym, we have a list of rules on a chalkboard on one of the side walls. The rule that is number one on the list is 'never say 'can't or cannot''. If someone does during one of their first classes, we simply show them the rule. Any infraction after that is twenty-five burpees on the spot. In our setting at the gym, those two words do not exist. Within realistic reason, there are no challenges or obstacles that can't be overcome. I try to instill this idea during classes, that yes, even though you're exhausted, you *can* push through and finish that set of reps, you *can always* do more than you think you can.

After my open-heart surgery to install a mechanical valve, I was having a difficult time doing a lap around the hospital wing with people assisting me. At that point, the idea of attempting an Ironman race, let alone finishing one, was so far off. The risk of health complications was at the forefront of my mind. The amount of work, commitment and absolute dedication that would be required was incomprehensible. The mental barriers were even harder to overcome. But in the end, my burning desire to accomplish that goal was enough to combat the adversity that was stacked against me. The countless workout and training sessions were grueling, to say the least. The challenge of looking from recovery to racing was harder still. Through all of this, what got me through was keeping that final goal in mind. Knowing that the risks I was taking would eventually pay off helped me to stay on course. This is proof that no matter how great the risk, no matter what barriers stand in the way, everyone can make their dreams a reality. Acknowledging that the risks and barriers are worth it serves as the first step on the journey to success.

When I first dreamed of opening up a fitness studio, that's all it was, a dream. A goal that was out of reach with an unfathomable amount of obstacles in between. However, that's because I was looking at it the wrong way. Once I started benchmarking the things I needed to do into manageable chunks, time flew by. Instead of trying to put everything together in one go, I took small steps, one by one. The next thing I knew, I was turning the key to open Jeremy's Boot Camp. If at first you don't succeed, reexamine your approach. Try an alternative action, or break the goal into smaller increments. Sometimes 'point A to point B' plans need a few pit stops along the way. But never give up, never back down, and everyone can leave their mark in their respective communities. Anyone can become an inspiration for countless others.

Jay Hauser

"There really is no one like Jeremy. He has been my best friend for years now, and even though I am older, he is the one I look up to. He is my inspiration. When I'm having a tough time during a workout or at work, I think about what he's been through and know that I have no excuses. He is the type of best friend everyone should have, he drives me to be better at everything I do. Without trying, he takes you outside of the box with everything, no matter what it is. Jeremy has so many different aspects to him; he is a father, husband, two-time open heart surgery survivor, black belt, Ironman, coach, business owner, trainer, but most importantly, my best friend. And he is the best example of all of these different aspects. I couldn't ask for a better best friend, just as his clients couldn't be in the hands of a better trainer and coach. If you're lucky enough to know him personally, you are blessed."

During the start of my campaign to raise money for the Nature Conservancy, we set a huge, lofty goal. I was told by many that I was wasting my time with such a high goal, and that I would be lucky if I hit five thousand dollars in fundraising. But almost $200,000 later, those same people are being proved wrong. One can never afford to listen to others' negativity, it's toxic. If I had let all of the doubt and negative talk get to me, I wouldn't have had nearly the same results I did. I could have allowed it to bother me or to feed into it. I simply nodded my head, said, "We'll see" and cruised past it.

Even though its cliché, the golden rule of 'treat others the way you want to be treated' is an excellent rule to live by. When someone is down, pick them up. Being obnoxious and disrespectful to others, in my opinion, is inexcusable. Disrespect is a pet peeve of mine. Seeing the way some people treat our elder citizens, women and our veterans, people who deserve nothing but the utmost respect, is nothing short of shameful. Typically, these people who are being disrespectful are the ones that are lacking the most in confidence and have insecurity issues. This is all the more reason that inspiring and motivating others is vital in any community.

I've always tried to do the right thing and make the right decisions. This really comes down to living and leading by example. In the physical fitness industry, in order to be successful, I have to eat, sleep and breathe the idea of leading by example. No one wants to be trained by someone who sets a poor example. No one is going to go into a facility that is run down, and no one is going to be inspired by someone who doesn't live that inspirational example every day. Thick skin is a necessity. The individuals that have been doubters and naysayers actually end up having the opposite effect from what they intended. These comments and doubts keep my fire burning at all times. Not a day goes by that I don't think about the people that have doubted me and the uncertainty they have expressed. When I am on a run, bike ride or swim, I sometimes think of the people that have bad-mouthed me or my endeavors, and I use it to motivate myself to push harder through the workout. At the same time, there is not a day that goes by that I don't think about and cherish the people that have believed in me and pushed me to be the best that I can. These people also fuel the fire and make me want to succeed, to show them that they are completely right to believe in me.

I remember one point in middle school that relates to this, and this moment was a turning point for me with my outlook on life. In class, a person came up to me during an activity that I was struggling with and said, "You're not going to amount to anything." For a split second, I believed them. I was struggling with class work that others were breezing through. But then I steeled myself and told him off. I knew I would make it in life, and I wasn't going to let anyone tell me otherwise. From that point on, I haven't put any stock in negative input from anyone.

It was in my high school years that I had a great work ethic instilled in me. Growing up playing basketball taught me the value of working together. I had the great fortune of being guided by some great coaches. Three coaches that gave me lots of life lessons were Coach Joe Drinon, Coach Frank Alosa and Coach Frank Monahan. Coach Alosa is also my uncle, so we were able to have extra training sessions here and there at my parent's house and his place. These sessions were often very intense, and included physical drills that were more conditioning than basketball-oriented.

There was one drill that he called, 'raider intensity'. Raider intensity meant that it was on, and giving any less than 110 percent was unacceptable. To this day, I still use the idea of raider intensity in my own training and during my fitness classes. If I'm having a tough day, I'll use raider intensity during a workout to get the frustration out. I use it in triathlons and I use it in martial arts. This idea of turning up the heat and going all in that I attained from my uncle has become a staple in my personal and work life.

In the hospital after my mechanical valve surgery, I was thinking about how I could get a bigger audience from the community to get involved in fitness. I wanted to get people more integrated with their own communities. By doing that, I hoped to have a snowball effect and have those individuals inspire more people to do the same. Sure enough, Concord has become a community that is very supportive and hands-on in relation to fitness. People that thought they couldn't do anything to make a difference in the community are now making a huge impact and paying it forward. Leaving impressions is what this life is all about. The bigger an impression you leave and the more people you affect, the more you will be remembered and cherished. I challenge everyone to go out and make a difference in their community. Whether it is through being a part of a non-profit, coaching a sports team, or just being a good role model for others to model and follow, everyone can and should make a lasting difference. That is how to live life to the fullest and how to live life to the fittest.

Chapter Nineteen
Post-Ironman Races

After finishing an Ironman race, I knew I could do nearly any other race I wanted to. But after training for so long and working so hard, I needed a bit of a break from the heavy training. I took several weeks of rest and relaxation following Ironman in 2010. Even though I was winding down from the part-time job of Ironman training, I certainly wasn't lounging around on the couch with chips, soda and television all day. I still ran, swam and biked, but toned all of it down from the intense workouts I had been used to.

There was the Medtronic Road Race coming up in just over two months, so I started focusing on this for my training. I was already in shape to run the ten-mile race, so I just had to maintain my fitness level for the race in October. Brook and Elli were excited for the vacation that Medtronic was providing us. An all-expenses paid trip to Minneapolis with cash to spend when we arrived was certainly an extremely generous gesture from the company that made my mechanical heart valve. Two months of running ensured that I was prepared for the road race, and before we knew it, we were off to Minneapolis.

To be in that amazing city representing an amazing company was such an experience. One of the best moments from that trip was when all twenty-five of the Medtronic Global Heroes were invited to the manufacturing building and shown how the mechanical valves and other medical equipment were all made. We then had a lunch where I was able to meet all of the other Global Heroes. They were from all over the world, and every person was amazing, just like the company I was surrounded by in '*Flat Line to Finish Line*', the film made by Ironheart. To this day, I still keep in touch with several of my fellow racers from this event.

After experiencing all Minneapolis had to offer, the day of the road race came. The morning was a beautiful one, with the car thermometer reading a cool 32 degrees, which I learned was typical Minneapolis weather for October. There was not a cloud in the sky, and the sun poured down onto us, making the temperature a bit more bearable. When I got to the starting line, I found several of my Medtronic teammates. We were all going to be wearing Global Heroes uniforms or t -shirts during the race. From the minute I greeted my teammates, I noticed that other racers were coming up to us and shaking our hands and thanking us. There were banners celebrating the Medtronic Global Heroes and listing some of our statistics. The outpouring of support this city was giving to this great cause, and to be able to be a part of it all was so touching.

The race started and we were off. I wasn't going to try to book it to the finish. There was so much to take in and enjoy during the run. A few miles into the race, the crowds were absolutely insane, dwarfing the energy level and volume of the crowds at Ironman. Every time someone from the crowd saw my Medtronic shirt, they waved and shouted, 'Thank you!' at me as I ran by. Many spectators held out their hands hoping for a high five, which I returned as often as I could. The crowd was supportive, as were my fellow racers. The whole race was so unique from any other race I have ever taken part in.

During the race, I got to know one of my fellow Global Heroes. His name was Larry, and he was a sort of hometown hero of the race. He was from Minnesota, and was also a recipient of a mechanical valve replacement. During the race, we talked and grew close, just like Bill and I had during the marathon log of Ironman. After the race, he invited Brook and me to his house for dinner with him and his family. We didn't have any plans set in stone for that night, and were excited to accept his offer.

Dinner with Larry and his family was such a great experience. He introduced us to his wife and kids before we gathered in his kitchen. Brook and I felt so welcomed in his home. The stories and laughter we shared that night were a great way to top off our stay in Minnesota. Larry and I formed a great relationship throughout that day, and still keep contact. Before leaving Minnesota, Larry decided he would visit us in New Hampshire the following year. I suggested that we do a road race when he came up, and he loved the idea. With a twinge of regret, we bid farewell to Minneapolis and headed home with many excellent memories.

A month rolled by after the wonderful experience in Minneapolis, and November was in the air. Two days before Ironman Lake Placid, I had received a ticket for the New York City Marathon, which would be taking place in early November of 2010. Similar to Ironman, we were provided with a hotel room that was only a few miles from the venue for the marathon. Brook and I were beyond grateful that so many gracious people had provided us places to stay in these past months during our trips.

Brook, Elli and I arrived at the hotel the night before the race. We settled in, tucked Elli in to bed, and then followed suit ourselves. After a good night's sleep and an excellent hotel breakfast we made our way to the course for the marathon. Even though it was November, it was much warmer on that day than it had been in Minneapolis in October for the Medtronic Race. The race went off without a hitch. The scope of the marathon was truly eye-opening. I knew it would be a bigger event than any race I had done before, but the sheer amount of people that came out to witness the marathon was astounding. Thousands of people packed the New York streets and sidewalks to get a glimpse of the racers as we jogged by. I ran one of my best runs ever that day, and crossed the finish line with a huge smile on my face. Even though I didn't have a Bill or a Larry for the race, it was a rewarding experience that I feel lucky to have done.

My wife drove my daughter and I back to the hotel following the race, where we planned to spend one more night before making our way back up to the Granite State. The sun was still high in the sky as we walked through the large double doors to the hotel, but we were all hungry for a big meal. Brook and I half-discussed, half-debated what the menu would be for dinner that night before I jumped in the shower to wash up. I had just put shampoo in my hair as I heard a shrill scream just as the bathroom door slammed against the wall.

"Brook! What's wrong?" I shouted as I partially ripped open the shower curtain to investigate. Thankfully Brook wasn't visibly hurt. She was holding Elli on her shoulder and looked very afraid. I was worried that something terrible had happened. Maybe someone had broken into the hotel room, or maybe something had happened in the hallway.

"There's..there's.. a cockroach in our room!" Brook screamed. She was seriously wigging out about this, jumping in place with her eyes darting everywhere. Now that I knew we weren't in any danger, I wrapped up the shower and started to pack up our bags. My parents weren't too far away from us at a casino in Connecticut. I called my mother and she answered just before it would have gone to voicemail. After explaining the bug situation and how uncomfortable Brook was about it, I asked, "Is there any way you guys can get us a room at the hotel you're staying at? We'll drive there right now if you can."

"Of course, Jeremy! It's not a problem. Let us know when you're here," she replied cheerily. We decided to forego dinner and eat with my parents once we got to the casino. Unfortunately for our stomachs, the two-hour drive time to the casino was doubled due to the traffic from the marathon. By the time we parked and called my parents to tell them of our arrival, we could barely hear each other over the growling from our stomachs. It turns out that holding off on eating was well worth it. The dinner we had was superb and was followed by some time in the casino. I'm not a big gambler, but I certainly had fun that night. Brook had a blast, and Elli was happy with the meal she had.

We had an awesome room to stay in that night. We got such good sleep that we decided to sleep in that next morning. Following a shower, we had an equally good breakfast before driving back home. This was the last big race I had planned for a while. After doing Ironman, the Medtronic Global Heroes Road Race and the New York Marathon all in five months, I wanted some time to wind down from all of it.

2010 became 2011, and I got a phone call from Larry in the spring. We had talked several times since the Medtronic race, and each time he voiced his desire to make his way to New Hampshire for a race. We finally settled on a road race being held in the northern part of the state during the first week of June. He arrived several days before the race and put himself up in a hotel. As the race loomed closer, the weather forecasts predicted unfavorable weather for that day. I told him about the crummy weather we were supposed to be having for race day, and even though he wasn't pleased, he was still on for running the race.

On race morning, I drove to Larry's hotel well before the sun was up. I picked him up at 3:30 on the dot and we started the hour drive up to the venue. On the way we caught each other up on all of the happenings in our lives. I told him that Brook and I were expecting our second child, to which he congratulated me profusely. He then responded with stories of his own kids back in Minnesota. There was never a lapse in the conversation; we just kept talking and talking, a testament to our relationship.

Driving up the highway to the venue, I noticed the thermometer on the dashboard gradually dropping. I had the windshield wipers on full blast as the rain came down in buckets. Sporadic gusts of wind didn't help my vision. Most of the drivers on the highway, including myself, were going well below the speed limit due to the horrible visibility from the storm.

When we were only five miles away from the venue, the temperature dropped yet again and the temperature display read a chilly 47 degrees. In the first week of June in New Hampshire, that is unheard of. Couple that with the pouring rain and I was starting to get antsy about the racing conditions. "Do we really want to do this, Jeremy?" Larry asked, concern creeping into his voice.

"Are you kidding? Saddle up, man. You flew here for this race. We're going through with it, Larry," I lightly scolded him. As we got closer, the temperature dropped even more, with no sign of the rain letting up at all. In the southbound lane of the highway, I could see that many vehicles had road bikes strapped to their roofs. I knew these must be racers that decided not to brave the weather, an option that was starting to look more and more inviting. Larry then asked me an off-hand question.

"Hey man, know of any good diners around here?" I was confused as to where that question came from.

"Uhm yeah, there's a really good one about twenty minutes from here," I answered. Just as I was about to ask why, Larry proposed a solution to the situation.

"How about this? We head to the diner, have an excellent meal, and head back after that. We'll tell everyone else we braved this insane weather, they won't know the difference either way." I mulled over the idea for a minute. My sensible thought process won out over my stubborn side, and I plugged in the diner to my GPS.

A half hour later, we were sitting in a cozy booth with warm mugs cupped between our hands. We quickly warmed up from the unusually cold weather out the window. Larry and I had meals fit for kings and spent the better part of three hours in the diner sharing great talk over great food. We learned from other racers that entered the diner that the race had ended up being delayed anyway, so we didn't feel as bad about our decision to opt out.

Following our feast, I gave Larry an abbreviated tour of northern New Hampshire and the beautiful scenery that the state has to offer. He was awestruck at some of the views I showed him, and thanked me for the sightseeing opportunity when we got back to his hotel. We embraced and promised to continue staying in touch with one another. Every time Larry calls me from Minnesota he asks if I've been back to the diner and how the weather is that day.

Since that not-so-gorgeous day, I've done several short races here and there: I've done more 5ks than I can count, completed a handful of half-marathons, over half a dozen marathons and participated in a few sprint-distance triathlons. Every event, regardless of size or length, has had memorable moments. Whether it is someone that I have met during the race or just an inspiring occurrence, every race has left a lasting impression on me in one way or another.

A perfect example of this is the 'Rock N Race' in Concord, New Hampshire. It is an annual event that I have competed in every year since 2006, barring the one year that I was struck with congestive heart failure. This race has the power to bring the entire community together and does so every year without fail when roughly six to seven thousand people come together to help raise money for cancer research and awareness.

For me, 2013 was the most memorable year of running this race. My best friend Jay Hauser had just lost his mother to brain cancer. My friends and I, including Jay, all ran and raised money in memory of his mother. This was a way to celebrate the life that his mother had enjoyed. She was an exceptionally wonderful woman and I will never, *ever,* forget some of the life lessons she taught me. We also decided during that race that from that point on, we would run in her memory.

Jay Hauser

"My mother passed away in the winter of 2013, and the Rock N Race was in the spring. My father, sister and I put together a team for the road race that year to honor her memory and to pay it forward to the hospital that cared for her. We decided to name the team, 'Bunnie's Bunch', since her nickname was Bunny. I put the word out to all of my friends and family about our team, our mission and the details of the road race. As I have come to expect, Jeremy was the first person to answer my call to support the cause. He helped with every step of organizing the team and put the word out to his own circle of connections. Seeing him there with no hesitation to support me meant the world to me. He always has my back, and he pulled through yet again with this road race."

"The road race, for me, served as a chance to reflect back on my mother's life and all that she believed in. She always loved Jeremy and loved that we were best friends. Our door was to open to Jeremy unequivocally, as she looked at Jeremy as family. She even supported his fundraising efforts for Ironman. The fact that I had an amazing best friend supporting and rallying behind the memory of an amazing woman...I can't begin to describe how it feels."

In 2012, I linked up with the Ironheart Foundation with the interest of managing and putting on a road race under their banner. They had recently put on a series of very successful road races in Washington state and I wanted to replicate that on the opposite coast. I contacted David Watkins and asked if I could organize a 5k race in the heart of Concord. He was happy to make it happen and pointed me in the right direction for logistics on how to go about setting up the race.

When I had come up with the idea of putting together a road race, I wanted to take the most enjoyable aspects of other races I had experienced and merge them all into one race. I dove into the work to put it together, finding that I actually enjoyed organizing all of the parts of the road race. I made sure we had excellent local vendors alongside great local sponsors. Within the 5k run, there would be a one-mile stretch that would serve as a time trial for the racers. Providing a sense of local togetherness was my ultimate goal with this 5k.

During that inaugural year I had a co-director for the Ironheart 5k, Christine Tatro. She was invaluable in the managing of the race. Christine and I worked very well together, and the experience was very smooth with her help. There was a lot to do leading up to the race. We had to find and select a local beneficiary for the race that would receive a portion of the proceeds, as well as work out details with vendors and performances from local groups. Both of us worked tirelessly to arrange all of these parts of the race.

Finally, race day came. A couple hundred people registered, an excellent turnout for our first year. It was a beautiful late spring day, partly cloudy with just the right breeze for a run. In addition to vendors and several demonstrations from local sources, we were lucky enough to have a series of demonstrations from Bodyworks Karate School in the park that day!

The race kicked off and the racers made their way out on to the course. Every ability level was represented. Some walked while others jogged, and still more sprinted out from the start. The race featured a beautiful flat course with the soothing downtown scenery. Overall, the race was a complete success. To top it all off, I was able to accomplish my goal of raising awareness about heart disease and bringing the community together through this race.

We have held the 5k on an annual basis since 2012 and have been blessed to have beautiful weather each year. Our sponsors and beneficiaries have helped greatly with the success of this road race. In the two most recent years, Brook and I have managed the race together. Concord has embraced the road race and provided excellent turnouts and excellent sponsors. It feels great to be able to run an Ironheart 5k in my town and to provide the community with awareness on heart disease.

In terms of triathlons or road races that I have done, it's never been about winning the race or trying to get a certain time. To me, it is more of an opportunity to celebrate the fact that I can do this, that I have a second chance at life. I could be six feet under right now, but since I'm not, I want to enjoy my experience in life. I just care about starting and finishing a race. If I have fun in between these two points, then I've won.

In Jeremy's Boot Camp, we have a large chalkboard on the side wall of the gym. There are always inspirational or comical quotes scribbled across the board, and I allow my clients to toss up some different ones from time to time. One of my favorites that I put up fairly regularly is, "'*Dead last'* beats '*did not finish'*, which trumps *'did not start.'*" This quote really relates to my outlook on racing. The numbers don't matter to me, for it's the experience that can't be quantified that is the real prize.

Since the New York Marathon, I hadn't done any races that were the same length or longer. That is, until I received an invite to run with former New England Patriot Tedy Bruschi's team in the 2015 Boston Marathon. I started training immediately and planned to put on a good show. I couldn't wait for the opportunity to run in such great company. Again, that's what matters in the end. I won't remember all of the split times and time-trial numbers from past races when I grow old. What I will remember are all of the great memories from my experiences.

Chapter Twenty
Community First, Business Second

I am one of the lucky individuals that lives the idea of, "If you love what you do, you'll never work a day in your life." My clients have always made my work fun and enjoyable. Since starting up my own gym, there has never been a day where I've woken up and thought, 'Darn, I have to go into work today and I'm not looking forward to it.' My work at the gyms that I have been a part of have been great, and I wouldn't change a thing. This is not to say that my experiences have always been a cakewalk.

In 2009, business started to pick up at the gym where I was leasing space from. My client base was growing, which led to more hours at work, and things were looking up. One snag in the upswing was that with more clients, they had more varied schedules that I had to try and fit in. These clients would go to me about hoping to get classes in at certain times, and unfortunately these were times I could not do due to my time that I had leased from the gym. I hated telling them that I couldn't conform to their schedule.

The next few years continued on a steady scale. Work was good, clients were good and life was good. I was working day and night to generate interest in my classes and to interest potential new clients, which proved to be a struggle. However, the more clients that were interested in my program, the more obvious it was that being constricted to the times that I was would not work for expanding my base of clients. After examining my options and crunching some numbers, I regretfully gave my notice to the gym in October of 2012.

At this time, I was completely unsure of the future. Brook and I were tossing the idea around of packing up and moving to the seacoast of New Hampshire, roughly an hour from our current home. This time was filled with questions and second-guessing. I questioned if I was doing the right thing. Should I get a consistent nine-to-five job in order to secure a consistent paycheck for my family? In order to get my head straight and figure out what was what, I sat down for an entire day and wrote down my thoughts and options. I wrote out all of my goals: family-related, work-related, physical goals and other miscellaneous endeavors I hoped to achieve in life.

During this brainstorming, I had noticed that if I could find a way to accommodate the various times clients wanted for classes, it could be something I could structure a business around. I figured out the number of clients a business like that would need to break even, how much we would need to pay the bills, and many other factors that would go into building, owning and running a successful fitness gym. Ultimately, by recognizing the interest in a different schedule for classes, I saw the potential for opening up a niche fitness gym catering specifically to individualized, hands-on fitness classes.

I sat down with Brook that night and we had one of the most intense conversations to date. We bounced ideas and opinions off one another and I relayed my ideas I had scribbled down earlier. I also pitched the idea of opening up our own business, an idea that she was on board with a lot more than I expected. During that discussion, we decided to stay rooted in Concord long enough to see if this business idea was palpable. If it worked out, we would stay in Concord. If not, we would explore the seacoast option at that time. We only have one life to live, and I wanted to take a risk that had a huge payoff potential in every way: financially, socially and physically. And the opening of this business was the answer.

That fall season, I always had something weighing on me. I had to juggle business options. There were a seemingly infinite amount of forms I needed to fill out. Research I had to do in order to ensure success in our business venture. There was no second chance with something as financially committing or as time-consuming as opening a fitness gym, so I wanted to be absolutely certain that I was as prepared as possible. Brook and I met with several business consultants and local experts. Following careful consideration and many changes of heart, we decided to take the plunge and start building a business.

This meant that we had also made the decision not to move and to stay in Concord. In November, we announced to the public that we were opening a fitness gym in the Concord area and gave a teasing glimpse of what the business would look like. We had several people show interest in signing up for classes before the business was even open, an excellent sign of promise.

During the process of getting the business up and running, my older brother Jeff was invaluable. As an adult, he had joined my dad and started working in the family construction business. During the first three months of initial construction, he was there all the time, working tirelessly. All of this while juggling the regular workload of the company's normal business! I was humbled by his help and couldn't have done it without him.

Word reached my ears about a little girl that was suffering from a heart condition at a very young age. This girl named Sophia was awaiting heart surgery in Massachusetts. I felt compelled to act on the situation and set up a fundraiser for her. In just two weeks, the community came together and raised almost two thousand dollars for her family. This event was certainly the highlight of that fall. Knowing that the community would respond in such a short time to help someone in need was so inspiring. I later learned that Sophia underwent a successful heart transplant and was released from the hospital in the winter months of 2014. After rallying with the community, I focused for the next year on my own project: to set up and run the best gym in Concord.

Winter of 2013 rolled around, and business plans started to become reality just as snow started to coat the frozen New England ground. During January of that winter, I started to worry about the business. Would we have enough people to keep the business open? How many additional staff will I need? How can I be sure I hire the right people for the job? What if I have too many people? What if I don't have enough? All of these questions were running marathons through my head. However, buzz was starting about the business and interest started growing. The months before the business would open turned to weeks. I was at the gym as much as I could be, helping with construction and other plans. The weeks until our grand opening turned to days.

And then the day came. On Saturday, March 9th, 2013, Jeremy's Boot Camp opened its doors to the public. The grand opening was a huge success. The support from the community was amazing. We were off to what seemed to be a strong start.

Two weeks into the business, I wasn't so sure about the direction of Jeremy's Boot Camp. I had a handful of one-on-one clients, along with ten or twelve people that had signed up for the group classes offered. I walked in that day to work and took my coat off as the door slid closed behind me. After removing my shoes, I walked over to the shoe rack to place them on the light-blue shelves. There were a total of three pairs of shoes. One of them was mine. I recognized Brook's running shoes next to mine. I didn't recognize the other pair, meaning it must belong to either one of our trainers or one of our members. I let out an audible sigh and shrugged my shoulders. I knew the business was taking off, but it was still brand-new, and would need time to take off and become the success I knew it could be.

Chapter Twenty-One

A Glimpse Into The Boot Camp Experience

19 Months After Opening

I put my right blinker on and applied pressure to the brakes as I neared the parking lot for Jeremy's Boot Camp. The building sits back from the road on a busy street in Concord. I pulled in to the lot and parked facing the gym. The date was October 20th, 2014. It was early evening and the crisp fall air nipped at my skin as I walked to the front entrance. Several trainers were already inside working with one-on-one clients.

The gym was brightly lit, with light bouncing off of the white and yellow concrete walls. I opened the door and the sounds of the gym poured out. Workout music was flowing through the gym. Our gym rules are posted just inside the doorway, the most important of which are 'Never say I can't', 'attitude is everything' and 'give 110% effort at all times!' Two of my employees looked up and waved to me as I slid my shoes off and tossed them in the shoe rack. I had a group class starting in a half hour, so I made my way through the gym to the back, where my office was located. As I walked through the gym I looked at the Jeremy's Boot Camp logo emblazoned on the wall. A pair of dog tags with our name hovers over four gold stars, with "Live Life to the Fittest!" written working out directly underneath it.

I hung my coat on the hooks behind my office door and dropped my bag underneath my desk. As is my custom, the first thing I did was look at the framed picture from my Ironman finish. Brook and I posed for the picture with an exhausted Elli clinging to Brook's arm for the photo. It's one of my favorite pictures of our family. Several other pictures that have been drawn by Elli and Bryn are displayed throughout the office, including a picture drawn by Elli that shows the four of us as stick figures. The top shelf in the office is littered with nutrition and fitness books of varying sizes. Directly below the books is another shelf with neatly labeled binders covering business and coaching topics. Bins of toys for Elli and Bryn sit directly next to my rolling office chair, which I sat down in to go over paperwork that needed tending to.

Fifteen minutes before the group class was set to start, I headed out onto the gym floor and greeted the clients that were already there. I make it a point to get to know my clients on a personal level. The more of a connection I can make with my clients and the better I get to know them, the more that both parties will get a better experience. The gym became more packed with clients as the minutes until class wound down. On the dot at 5:45, I started the class.

The class started with a quick bit of cardio to get into a rhythm and warmed up. I instructed them to do a mix of up-downs, side planks and jumping jacks on their own for two minutes, then we would get right into the stations we'd be using for the next part of the class. I looked out at the class members. I knew almost everyone in the class but saw one new face that night and made sure to go over, introduce myself and ensure her that she was in for a great class.

The amazing thing about the group classes at Jeremy's Boot Camp is the variety of individuals in the classes. There were tall, young, burly tattooed guys working next to lean, middle-aged women, and everything in between. Girls were right alongside guys, old was mixed with young, and Boot Camp veterans were working next to newcomers.

After everyone had warmed up, I called for their attention in order to explain the layout of the stations. The seven stations that night were as follows: 1. chin-ups or pull-ups, 2. jumping rope whip with a squat thrust in between, 3. push-up walks with a sliding pad for the feet, 4. work on the rowing machine, 5. kettle bell squats, 6. curling weights, and 7. holding a push-up position with feet on a large medicine ball. In groups of two, the class would be spending one minute per station and then take a thirty-second break before starting at the next station.

I walked over to the stereo, cranked the music up, hit the start button on the stopwatch and shouted, "Let's get going, go!" The gym suddenly came to life. The sound of the ropes smacking into the floor competed with the sound of the rowing machine. I walked around the class as everyone got into the groove of the workout. I am never stationary when teaching classes at the gym. I made a point to offer encouragement or coaching at each station before letting the class know it was time to switch to the next station.

The benefit to running stations in group classes is that the clients can cater the workouts to their own level. If a client can only do chin-ups, that's fine. But if they can do twenty pull-ups, that's also able to be done in the stations. Everything in my classes is able to be done at any fitness level. The clients can use different techniques and approaches at each station to fit their personal fitness level. This is what I feel sets Jeremy's Boot Camp apart, allowing clients to make progress on their own personal level without feeling rushed or held back.

By this point, the sound of labored breathing and grunts of effort started to become more audible. Short, friendly conversations could be heard during the thirty-second breaks in between stations. At our gym, the environment is such that everyone in class knows everyone else. I will even jump in and share some quick small talk from time to time during these breaks, asking my clients about their days or how their families are doing.

Before I knew it, the class was halfway done. I modified most of the stations to incorporate a different drill or activity and started the circuit over again. I amped up the music in the gym and gave more energy input to the clients. I believe that the difference between a good coach and a great coach is knowing how much energy input is needed in a class or a session. Too little energy input makes the coach seem disinterested, but too much energy is at best overwhelming and at worst unnerving. It takes a keen sense to know when to crank the music and when to provide more motivation to the class. I try to stay as conscious of the energy level as I can. After coaching and running classes for several years, it has become second nature to me.

Another important detail to know as a coach is your clients' limits. These people are coming to me to lose weight and get in shape, others are looking to train for something specific, and others are just looking for a great workout. Pushing someone or a group of people beyond their limit can be detrimental for everyone involved. On the other hand, workouts are not meant to be a cakewalk. Just like the energy level in a class, knowing the limits of my clients is absolutely essential to running this business successfully.

"You're halfway through the circuit, push yourself!" I shouted, encouraging the class to give it all they had, as they were nearing the end of class. Everyone in class was red-faced. Veterans of my class were sweating and panting just as much as the woman taking her first class. I walked to each station and gave each partner pair individual encouragement to keep going. I applauded during the thirty second break and commended the effort they were putting forth. "Alright, here it is, last station for this circuit, raider intensity right here, come on!" The whole class responded by grimacing in effort and going as hard as they could for the last minute of the circuit, which I applauded immediately after.

After that last station was finished, I switched the class to a less cardio-intensive workout as a break from the stations. I demonstrated partner push-ups and partner sit-ups. For partner push-ups, the groups would do a push-up together, followed by high-fiving each other while remaining in the push-up position. As for the partner sit-ups, the idea is to do sit-ups at the same time as one another with feet intertwined while passing a medicine ball back and forth. The groups did each exercise for one minute before taking a quick water break. I joked with the groups by saying, "every time you guys complete a push-up or sit-up, I want you to say, 'I love push-ups' or 'I love sit-ups'." This drew laughter and smiles from the class, lifting the mood.

My gaze traveled to the Ironman poster on the wall, hung next to our logo. The image captures the true nature of Ironman: hundreds of racers are in the water, but all that you can see is a maze of arms and red swim caps. White water is crashing all around the swimmers in the picture. Some faces are frozen in a wince of effort, their eyes covered in the glare of the tinted goggles. That picture serves as a constant reminder of what I have accomplished, and what everyone can accomplish if they truly wish to do so.

"Alright guys, here we go, last time through the circuit. This is it, then class is over. Give it all you've got right here, go!" I had turned down the music for the partner push-ups and sit-ups as a sign to take a breather, but break time was over, and I made sure the class knew that by throwing the volume knob on full. At this point, the woman who was in her first class raised her hand and said that she wasn't sure what to do at one of the modified stations. I explained what to do, and she replied that she wasn't sure if she could do it. After ensuring her she had it in the bag, she tentatively tried it, and sure enough, she rocked it! She actually was one of the best in the class at the exercise. This proves that you can always do more than you think you can. Oftentimes, all it takes is putting your head down and going for it.

Everyone in class had put the pedal to the metal; they were all pushing themselves and their partners. One group that I especially liked consisted of a big, tall, burly tattooed man and a lean, middle-aged woman. Not only was the woman keeping up with the much larger guy, but she was challenging him and pushing him to do more and keep up with her. And boy was he trying! This is the kind of situation that really represents the best of fitness gyms.

The heavy breathing was almost as loud as the music by the time the last station of the last circuit came around. I demanded nothing less than the best effort they had as I started the stopwatch for the last minute of the circuit. Everyone in class had drenched shirts. Their arms and faces were glistening with sweat as they pushed themselves. I counted down the last ten seconds of the workout as I surveyed the class. Everyone was either gritting their teeth or scrunching their eyes, a true testament to how honest of an effort they were all giving.

"Time! Excellent job guys, way to go. Let's circle up and stretch," I said as I joined in for the ending stretches. We all stretched together for two minutes before I dismissed the class. People were wiping their faces with towels or their own shirts. I approached the newcomer and asked how she liked her class. Through deep breaths, she said that she loved it as she flashed a genuine smile. I congratulated her on a great first class and wished her a good rest of the evening.

I looked out into the waiting area where most of the class had circled around the shoe rack, the unofficial social hub post-workout at Jeremy's Boot Camp. Everyone was socializing with one another as they put on clean shirts or took sips of water. It is always awesome to see a class go from total effort in a workout to them all being friendly and familiar with one another. Boot Camp is more than a collection of individuals looking to work out, it really is a close-knit community of great people that just happen to all work out together. Seeing all of our clients interact as they do always puts a smile on my face and assures me that this is a successful business, because to me, the impact that Jeremy's Boot Camp makes on the community is the most important measure of success.

Chapter Twenty-Two
Tedy's Team and the Boston Marathon

If there's one sport I enjoy watching, it's football. And living in New England, if there's one team I enjoy watching, it's the Patriots. I know that they're not exactly 'America's Team' (though their record is exceedingly better than 'America's Team'), but I'll always be a fan through and through. With that in mind, I remember when the Patriots began their meteoric rise during the turn of the century, with a bunch of huge names at the helm; Brady, Vinatieri, Wilfork, Bruschi, and other giant players. Tedy Bruschi, one of those massive names, would turn out to be a player very relatable to me; in 2005, mere days after winning the Super Bowl and playing in the Pro Bowl, Bruschi suffered a stroke due to something called a PFO (Patent Foramen Ovale), a congenital heart defect. This condition produces a hole in the heart, and can occur with no warning or history. After months of rehabilitation and medical care, Bruschi was back to work doing what he did best. But not before he and his wife reached out to the American Stroke Association, and in typical Bruschi fashion, sought out ways to give back to the community and raise awareness about stroke. In 2005, Tedy's Team was created.

After retiring from professional football in 2009, Bruschi continued to work in his community on raising awareness about stroke. With the formation of Tedy's Team, Bruschi now had a means to reach a far greater audience: the Boston Marathon.

Entering into the Boston Marathon can be done one of two ways: qualifying through specific marathons under specific (and grueling) time splits, or by fundraising a minimum amount. The first year Tedy's Team participated in the Boston Marathon, the team had secured five racing spots due to fundraising , with the proceeds going to support stroke and heart disease awareness, research, education and advocacy. The team has only grown from there.

While I could only slightly relate to Tedy at the time he suffered the stroke (he suffered his setback two years before I experienced my second case of heart failure, and I hadn't competed in Ironman yet), I certainly can now. It was hard enough for me to recover from my surgery and compete in Ironman. But when I learned about how Tedy had recovered from his stroke to not only get back to where he was on a Super Bowl caliber team, but to then *get better* than he had been before, I was blown away. He had climbed back to the peak of football greats, and continued to improve. Talk about inspiration!

I was introduced to Tedy's Team back in 2014 by a friend of mine who was very involved in the running scene. After some quick research of the team, I knew it was something I wanted to be a part of, especially because of the cause Tedy was running for, which was literally near and dear to my heart. I called a member of Tedy's Team whose name I recognized as an acquaintance of mine and asked him how I could go about applying to join. Once I saw that the team centered around running events, especially, the Boston Marathon, I was over the moon! Sure, I had run other marathons, and at their core all marathons are the same basic formula (26.2 miles of running, start on one line and cross the other), the Boston Marathon is world renowned.

The Boston Marathon is the oldest annual marathon in the world. Even though Tedy and the Patriots are loved by New England, the Boston Marathon boasts a larger draw, pulling in over 500,000 spectators every year for their one event. The event has averaged a little over 30,000 entrants over the past few years. That number is just staggering. Of those entrants, about a fifth are those running for charity.

I knew that I couldn't get into the Boston Marathon based on time. Today, the qualifying time for my age group is just over three hours. To save you the math, that's a running pace of just under seven minutes per mile. That is the *pace.* The level of conditioning one needs to be able to keep a sub-seven-minute mile pace for a marathon is insane. Nevertheless, the entry spots for the Boston Marathon based on time get snatched up in less than a day once registration opens. To even qualify for the Boston Marathon on running credentials alone is a feat in and of itself. For charity runners, there is a six-hour cutoff time during the marathon, nearly doubling the time to complete the race versus a runner entering on running time.

My interest in Tedy's Team combined with the fact that they ran the Boston Marathon as charity runners was too good to pass up. Their mission aligned with my outlook and goals, and I applied to become a part of the team in the summer of 2014. I wasn't sure if I would get accepted, and would anxiously check my phone and email several times a day, hoping to find a voicemail or email congratulating me. Several weeks later, I was rewarded with an acceptance email saying I was now a part of the 2014/2015 Tedy's Team!

For official Boston Marathon charity runners, the minimum fundraising amount to start is $5,000. On Tedy's Team, our individual minimums are $7,500, with an ultimate goal of raising more. However, we have been blowing that goal out of the water lately; in 2019, Tedy's Team raised an astounding $737,000 for stroke and heart disease research, education, awareness and survivor assistance, with that fundraising contributed to by 46 members!

One of the biggest fundraising events I have a hand in regularly is a local charity basketball game with the Harlem Wizards, a professional team whose focus is entertainment and bringing the 'wow factor' to a crowd. We have held this event once a year for the past four years at Bishop Brady, my high school. Despite the fact that the Harlem Wizards are the big draw in the fundraising aspect, the best part is the team they play against; pillars in our community. The community of Concord has always come together for this event, with the 'average joe' team consisting of law enforcement, big names in the community, and even several governors over the years. These individuals also contribute directly to the fundraising as well as advertise the event, exponentially increasing the success and draw the game produces. We have even had Tedy as our coach, twice!

The best part about this event is that while it is a fundraiser, it engages all aspects of our community and brings everyone together for a good time. I have a blast playing on my old court that I spent so many hours on when I was a kid. The small business owners, leaders and heroes of our community all come together and have fun. But the best part for me is seeing the fun that the audience has. The smiles and gasps and cheers from the kids in the crowd is why I've chosen to repeat this fundraiser over the years. The game is fun for both kids and adults to watch. And when I go to pick up my daughters from school on the days following the game and see all of the Harlem Wizards jerseys walking out of the school, it brings a swell of pride up.

Each year, approximately six months go into planning and fundraising for the Boston Marathon from the team members, with several non-racing staff members working full time and year round to make everything run smoothly. With all of us having full-time jobs, families and everything else in our lives to tend to, fitting in all the additional effort that fundraising and training calls for is no small task.

As the day of the race gets close, Tedy's Team hosts a team dinner on the Saturday before the marathon every year, deemed our 'Night of Inspiration' dinner. The dinner is held in Boston. It's our way to celebrate all the work and time we have put in to get to this point. Not only that, but it serves to remind us why we do what we do.

A survivor or caregiver will speak at the dinner; telling their stories, showing their scars and reflecting on their own journeys. While each story is unique, all of us on Tedy's Team relate in some way to the struggles or obstacles that every team member has faced. Awards are given out during the dinner, and the pinnacle of the camaraderie always comes when our team leader and founder stands to make his own speech. I can imagine that Tedy was really able to rile up the locker room with the Patriots, because by the time he is done with his speech I am ready to charge head on into anything. The night helps us put everything into perspective and gives us an appreciation for everything we are able to do. After the group photos and socializing at dinner, it's time for the Boston Marathon. The day of the marathon is chalk full with travel, waiting, planning, waiting, running (obviously), and then some more waiting. The morning usually starts around three or four in the morning. Some years I have been able to stay with friends down in Massachusetts the night before the marathon to cut down on travel time. Regardless, I would jump on a bus that would take me into Hopkinton, Massachusetts. By the time my morning routine was done, coffee had been inhaled and the bus ride was done, the sun would be creeping over the horizon, greeting me as I got off of the bus around seven in the morning. From there, we meet as a team at a business that belongs to a stroke survivor that donates their location every year. Tedy's Team provides breakfast foods to share along with coffee and water. From there, the waiting game begins, which we fill by socializing, sharing more stories and getting each other psyched for the experience that is to come. Many times, the conversation moves to prior marathon stories, of which I have plenty.

In 2016, I had the pleasure of running with my little brother. He trained so hard for the race, and to be able to run with him at my side was one of the best experiences of my life. That year, the weather was great for the marathon; a cool breeze, not too humid and partly cloudy. I can't say the same about the past two years., 2018 and 2019. 26.2 miles in torrential rain and wind is certainly humbling.

The Boston Marathon, having tens of thousands of participants, breaks down the racers into waves. First are the wheelchair racers starting around 9 am, then the handcycles and duos about twenty-five minutes later. The elite men and elite women follow about eight minutes after that. Next, the para athletic division is up, usually ten minutes before 10 am . Finally, the rest of the racers are broken into four waves, staggered twenty-five minutes apart from one another. This breakdown is necessary to avoid overcrowding on the course. Historically, Tedy's Team has run in wave four.

As our start time creeps closer, we pack everything up from our tailgating session and walk to the starting line, which happens to only be about a block away from the house. There is a constant and heavy stream of foot traffic, which only serves to amplify our nerves. As we walk through the gate on a side street at the start, Tedy and Heidi (Tedy's Team Co-Founder and Tedy's wife) high five and hug all of us on the team. Once through the gate and onto the gated area, it is about a half mile walk to the actual starting line. Once I pass through that gate, a switch somewhere in me flips every year. Something about walking into the area that only the racers go makes everything click into place. I start getting into the mental space I need to be in for the race. Excitement, anticipation and eagerness are all crashing into each other as they flow through my mind, along with the bombardment of noise from the crowd.

It feels like the center of an amphitheater, with thousands of people crammed against the gates. Signs are waved back and forth and pictures are snapped on phones as friends, family, coaches and general spectators all intermingle, jostling for a view of the start line.

What strikes me every year at the starting line is the company that I know I am surrounded by, and I don't just refer to my team. Wave four is made up of the charity runners . As I look around at all of the unfamiliar faces, I know that every one of them has not only done the same caliber of training that I have but has worked hard at fundraising to get where we were all standing. It is a large dose of humble pie, knowing the selflessness that I am surrounded by every year.

Each year, above the crackling energy of the racers and the roar of the crowd, is the whir of helicopters circling above us. Snipers are positioned on rooftops around the course. Law enforcement can also be seen patrolling the grounds, ensuring everyone's safety. I think I speak for everyone when I say thank you to all of our law enforcement that keep this beloved race safe.

As we stand at the start line, I am able to relate to sardines in a can. Thousands of us are nearly shoulder to shoulder. The fact that all of us are trying to stay loose and want to start running doesn't make the surroundings any more comfortable. The audible countdown to the start of the race is the most welcome sound of the day. "Five, four, three two one…" ***POP!*** I practically leap into my first stride, thankful to be moving but making sure to pace myself in the first downhill section. I can't help but smile as I start the race. Surrounded by my teammates, I gaze up into the sky as I start to find my rhythm and think of my dad, knowing that he is watching over me and smiling just as wide.

Chapter Twenty-Three
The Question of Tomorrow

Mr. Hardy

"Jeremy has been an elite athlete since the day I met him, and he has only improved over time. He has an extremely high degree of self-accountability, which directly correlates to the award-winning success of his business. He fully embodies his martial arts lifestyle just as he embodies his endurance sports. Jeremy is truly someone to look up to, and you'll never meet anyone else quite like him."

The first six months after we opened Jeremy's Boot Camp dragged by. I would go days with no sleep, as I was swamped with Boot Camp related work. Calculating financial information, running classes, marketing, cleaning and scheduling times for clients took up all of my attention and energy. I was constantly pulling fifteen hour work days with late nights on the weekend to ensure that the business was as well maintained as possible.

My background experiences from other areas of my life helped with my work during the initial months of running my own gym. Martial arts had taught me to never give up and to keep pressing on, no matter how much adversity was in my way. Endurance sports had shown me how to keep an aggressive pace, and I translated these traits into my business plan. I worked hard to develop unique advertising for the gym by offering irresistible deals and discounts for membership and getting the word out to the community that an innovative new gym was in town.

We celebrated six months of business in the fall of 2013. Business had started to pick up at that point. There were established group classes, with additional classes and times being added to the schedule. The amount of one-on-one clients were also growing in numbers, so much that I was considering hiring more trainers and staff to accommodate the demand. Another noteworthy figure from this time was our retention rate: it was much higher than expected. I pulled Brook aside one night at home and showed her the numbers. Her eyebrows rose at the retention rate the gym had at that time. This reinforced my business plan. Our clients were happy with the format we provided and seeing this retention rate served as lighter fluid to fuel my business fire.

We were doing pretty good at our six-month mark. I was pleased with the numbers and quality of the business but wanted to take Jeremy's Boot Camp from good to great. At the six-month mark, I implemented a new feedback system designed for fitness studios. It was a way in which I could gauge the growth of the business in every form and on every spectrum. Through this system, I would learn the good, the bad and the ugly about running a gym.

Jay Hauser

"Jeremy and I recently ran a half marathon together. I was running this half marathon in memory of my mother, and when I asked Jeremy to join me, he was on board before I finished my sentence. Even though we always push each other, he is a far better runner than I am, so I knew he would finish before me. He had gotten ahead of me halfway through the thirteen mile race."

"As I dragged myself up to the nine mile marker, I saw Jeremy waiting for me. I was completely surprised. When I asked him what he was

doing, he told me, "My time doesn't matter, man. Running these last miles with you and crossing the finish line together is what matters." Sure enough, we finished the race together."

"This goes to show what an amazing person he is. Normally, racers are very focused on the numbers. Not Jeremy. He stood by his best friend and pushed me to finish the rest of the race. To this day, I get choked up talking about it. I will never be able to express how much that act meant to me."

For the rest of 2013, I set up benchmark numbers: class attendance, one-on-one clients and the amount of new members at the gym all had benchmark numbers for us to aim for. These numbers were set up on a monthly basis. To my surprise and excitement, we hit or surpassed every benchmark for every month leading up to 2014. Due to the amazing numbers from that year, I set some really high expectations for 2014 as related to attendance per month, quarterly and for the whole year.

The expectations for 2014 were high, but our drive was higher. We repeated the success of the previous year, and then some. We hit the mark I had set for annual attendance...in September. We had grown every month that year. The summer months are slow times for most physical fitness businesses, as people are relaxing on vacations or participating in other activities. But not here at the Boot Camp. We kept growing, and there's no sign of slowing down. September of 2014 was our highest month ever for new member sign-ups. I can't count the amount of times I have had clients come up to me and say how much they enjoy the atmosphere we provide at the gym.

This atmosphere that we provide is made and maintained by our staff of fantastic trainers. They take care of their clients and put their needs and concerns above all else. These trainers have always shown nothing but the utmost professionalism. They work to keep the showers, gym floor and equipment spotless. I want our clients to be wowed the first time they walk through our door and every single time after that. Thanks to our staff, the experience our clients get here is like no other. Having talked with people who have come here from other gyms, I know that what we offer is unique. We're not just a machine factory with televisions on the walls. Jeremy's Boot Camp is a place to change one's life and to leave as a better person than when first entering the gym.

One thing that stands out to me about the gym is all of the different backgrounds that people come from. Everyone in here has their own life story, and they are all so different from one another. We have lawyers, government officials, school teachers, construction workers, retail managers, real estate brokers, students and everything in between. The idea that all of these different professions, all with different reasons for being here, can come together and take part in the same group class puts a big smile on my face. I am pleased to say that this is similar to my experience at Bodyworks during my classes there. Everyone at karate has such a different story than everyone else in class, but they are brought together by their common bond of the martial arts. The same rings true for our clients here at the gym.

When I opened the gym, my goal was to do more than provide the community with a place to get a good workout. My goal was to help people change their lives. To hear our clients come up to us and tell us exactly how their membership at the gym has positively influenced their lives is so gratifying. We have had multiple clients that have lost over one hundred pounds. Some clients have come in the door on blood pressure medications that no longer need it after being a part of our classes. Many of our clients have run local 5ks that had never dreamed of such a feat before coming into Jeremy's Boot Camp. A handful of our members have hit the 1,000-class mark with us! We even have one client currently training for a half-Ironman race that hadn't run any type of race before getting her gym membership here. People come in and change their lives for the better. We just provide the facility and the means to do so.

Marshall Crane

"Jeremy was one of the first people that I called when I moved back to the Boston area. He answered right away, and after exchanging small talk I told him how I wanted to get back into shape. I had been an elite athlete with a cut physique and wanted that to be the case again. He asked me to come and visit him at his new gym, Jeremy's Boot Camp. I was excited to see what he had built for a business and, knowing Jeremy, came prepared to work out."

"After getting a tour of the entire gym, he and I sat down and discussed details of a workout program for me. He set a hefty schedule for me as a one-on-one class with him. In fact, I only made it fifteen minutes into the first workout with him before running outside and throwing up in the parking lot. Nevertheless, I came back determined the next time. I made it twenty minutes before history repeated itself."

"I slowly got back into the shape I had been in during my twenties. One year after that initial meeting with Jeremy, I am in the best shape of my life. I recently competed in and completed the Tough Mudder race in Massachusetts, a grueling race that pushed me to my limit. But thanks to Jeremy, my limit was high enough that I made it through. Jeremy really isn't one in a million. He blows away everyone that is considered one in a million; this guy is easily one in a billion."

I am so thrilled that that the business has achieved what it has to this point. Our new member rate reinforces that Brook and I did the right thing when we made the decision to stay local and work on the gym. After our amazing degree of success over the past six years, I have decided to start exploring expansion options. I started laying out some long-term (10 year) business goals in 2015, some of which relate to expanding the business to multiple locations.

We are working on licensing the 'Live Life to the Fittest' trademark in order for other gyms and facilities to be able to use it in their own marketing if they incorporate our programs. In the future, we are aiming to be involved in some way or another with fifty different locations. If our prior success is any indicator, I am sure that we will hit that mark.

Currently, we are in the process of potentially opening up a second location as a licensed facility. We have one person with a contract in hand and are very close to solidifying a final deal. We are just getting started with our huge plans for expansion, with this being the first step. I have already fallen in love with looking at how we can take our business and put it into different aspects of different communities. Just as we are in Concord, I want our future locations to be a staple in their respective communities. As a business owner, I feel that it is important to strive to be a pivotal moving component of the communities we are a part of.

Since the very first days of being open, it has always been important to me that the gym be community oriented. We have kept with our founding ideals and are still just as involved in the Concord community as when we opened. We have aimed to keep doing what we have been doing, as we've had success with our innovative approach to getting an excellent workout.

One day in 2014, I got driven by my friend Jay to a meeting that was being held announcing me as the 2014 Concord Young Professional of the Year. I was speechless as I received the award. A piece was done on the gym for the local newspaper, and the feedback has been completely positive. This goes to show that by giving back to the community, has its own ways of returning the favor.

Everything Brook and I have been through has happened for a reason, and that reason is to be where we are today. We have a beautiful family, a beautiful house and a beautiful business. All of this is why we did what we did, to be happy. The weeks upon weeks of no sleep and stress-filled days where it seemed like I was trying to push through a brick wall were all to get to where Jeremy's Boot Camp is today. We have well over two hundred members at our Concord facility, and this number is increasing on an exponential basis.

The shoe rack that only had three pairs of shoes during the introductory weeks is now overflowing. More often than not, I need to put my non-workout shoes in my office because there is simply no room on the shoe rack. That rack has been a visual measure of the success of our business. We actually needed to put a second shoe rack in to accommodate all of the eager members coming in to work out.

During the beginning of October 2014, I was contacted via email and informed that Jeremy's Boot Camp had been selected as the 2014 MindBody Bold Business of the year. This award was bestowed upon Jeremy's Boot Camp for being an innovative force in the fitness industry, and we were honored to receive this nomination and award. To me, this reinforced that we were making an impact with our gym and providing more than just a place to burn calories and get fit. We are providing a place to burn calories, get fit, and change your lifestyle.

In the Ironheart documentary in which I am part of the cast, one of the trailers portrayed each of us as certain characters. David was given the title of 'the leader' while another was called, 'father figure'. As for me, I was referred to as 'the dreamer'. The title certainly fits me. Ever since I was a young boy, I have dreamed up ideas or goals, seen the working parts of the situation and tried to see the potential obstacles that I would be facing. This means eliminating the negativity from nay-sayers about these dreams.

Dreams are funny things. By dreams, I don't mean your brain's imagination when sleeping; I mean the lofty goals in one's life. In my opinion, you can do one of two things with your dreams in life: either keep them to yourself and never tell anyone about them, or you can put them down on paper and put that paper somewhere where you'll see them every day. This way, the idea keeps building from the constant exposure. You build off of this idea, over and over, day after day, week after week. If managed properly, these dreams start to become food for thought. You start to realize that they are possible the more you work at taking baby steps toward the final goal. Before you know it, these dreams can and will become reality.

Brook Woodward

"He always aims high with everything he does, no matter how big or small the obstacle. And no matter how much he has going on, Jeremy has always put his family first. Through all of his training and work with the gym, he always manages to be as involved with the girls as possible. He goes to their dance recitals, he involves them in his training, and it's so touching to see how much he cares about them."

This is exactly how I have operated my whole life. My wife always tells me, "Jeremy, you're such a dreamer. No matter what, you always have high hopes and so many dreams." She's right on the mark. The only way to get to a new level of success in life is to dream. I think that if I don't have a dream to chase that I'm not living life correctly. Once I complete or accomplish one dream, I focus on another dream. This idea translates to every aspect of my life. I have dreams in relation to triathlons, my business and my martial arts training.

When I was in the hospital recovering from my second open-heart surgery in 2007, I realized how many things I had taken for granted. The harsh reality that tomorrow is never guaranteed settled in while I was in recovery. Knowing that I had been given a new lease on life, I wanted to make sure that I lived out as many of my dreams as possible. I realized that I had many dreams, so many that I wanted to keep track of all of them in one spot.

One day while relaxing after doing laps around the recovery floor, I wrote down a bucket list of sorts. Instead of making a list to encompass my entire life, I put a timeline of twenty-five years on the list. The doctors had told me that on average, a mechanical heart valve recipient goes twenty-five to thirty years before requiring corrective surgery to repair the valve. With the time this valve had given me, I came up with a bucket list of everything I wanted to do in life over that time.

This list had everything on it, both quantifiable goals and goals that couldn't be measured. Being a better person, being more community involved, being an elite triathlete by completing an Ironman race, getting my fourth degree in Kenpo and continuing my Kung Fu training, saving money for a family, having a family and being a great Dad were all items on the list, even meeting my sister that I've never met. All in all, there were about forty items. One noticeable subject not on this list were things people were telling me I should do, such as a certain road race or competition. I wanted to have big, broad goals to reach. To me, success is not defined by what you have, but rather *how* one has lived their life.

Once I went home from the hospital, I made a copy of the list, adding several items to the long note. There were all kinds of crazy items on the final list. It wasn't about 'I want this', or 'I want to buy that'. As I reviewed it, I noticed that they all had a common theme: all of these wishes were dear to my heart. There was nothing on the list that was a new experience or concept, but rather wishes that I could better myself or expand my experience in certain areas of my life.

I folded the list and put it into a fancy sealed box. I slid it into my pocket, made my way downstairs and told Brook that I was going for a light run. Once I was outside, I grabbed a small garden shovel and jogged my way to Bear Brook State Park and walked the trails. It was a beautiful fall day. The leaves had just started to change color, signaling that winter was just around the bend. It was a rather warm day for fall, as my sweaty tank top and shorts attested to.

I took in the scenery and beautiful day as I walked through one of the main trails in the woods. I didn't have any certain spot in mind, so I just walked, taking in the scenery. At one point, I heard a brook running next to the trail. I was curious and left the path to investigate. I made my way through a maze of trees for a minute before stumbling upon the brook and almost stepping in it. The trickling stream snaked through the woods and past several large boulders nestled under the trees. I saw a large tree several feet downstream that towered over its neighbors. I walked over to it and leaned into the trunk, slid down the smooth bark and sat between the large roots.

After relaxing and enjoying the nature scene laid out all around me, I hoisted myself up and pulled out the small shovel. I took several steps toward the small brook and dug a shallow hole in the ground. I removed the box from my pocket and rubbed the cover, allowing myself to zone out while staring at the box. Once I snapped out if it, I knelt down and placed the box gently into the hole, as if the it might break if I mishandled it. In addition to the dirt I had shoveled out, I covered the hidden gem in leaves and bits of gravel from my immediate surroundings.

To this day, I have not been back out on the nature trails in Bear Brook. That mini-bucket list serves as my gauge of success in life. It is tucked away in a location only I know. Hopefully, once I undergo my next heart surgery in two decades, I can go back, unearth that list and see that I accomplished my goals. Sure, I will probably have gray hair. Maybe I'll have no hair. My daughters will have grown into amazing women. Jeremy's Boot Camp, if all goes well, will be a flourishing business. Twenty-five to thirty years in the future I plan to take that same walk, sit against that same tree, listen to the hypnotic rhythm of that same brook, and look back on this same life to see if I have truly lived life to the fittest.

About the Author

Jeremy Woodward

Jeremy Woodward is a 2x Heart Failure Survivor, author, motivational speaker, athlete, and host of the **Get Inspired With Jeremy** Podcast Show.

He has been featured in over 100+ media outlets that include: Sports Illustrated Online, CNN, ABC, Taekwondo Times and many more!

About the Author

Ben Veilleux

Benjamin Veilleux lives in New Hampshire with his wife and two sons. This is his second published book, and he has more on the way.

He is a fifth degree black belt in combined Kenpo and enjoys rock climbing in his spare time.

About the Publisher

Todd Civin

Todd Civin is a husband, father of five and grandfather of four. He is a graduate of Syracuse University Newhouse School of Public Communications. Todd is creator of Civin Media Relations and is the Social Media Director for the Kyle Pease Foundation & The Hoyt Foundation.

He has written and published nearly forty biographies and children's books to date and is proud to add Heart Failure to Victory to his publishing resume.

Made in the USA
Middletown, DE
24 December 2020